Being human

Being human

A Christian understanding of personhood
illustrated with reference to power, money, sex and time

*Report of the Doctrine Commission
of the General Synod
of the Church of England*

CHURCH HOUSE
PUBLISHING

Church House Publishing
Church House
Great Smith Street
London
SW1P 3NZ

ISBN 0 7151 3866 9

GS 1494

Published 2003 for the Doctrine Commission of the General Synod of the Church of England by
Church House Publishing.

Cover design by Church House Publishing

Printed in England by The Cromwell Press Ltd,
Trowbridge, Wiltshire

Contents

The Doctrine Commission 1996–2003

Chairman
The Right Revd Professor Stephen Sykes
Principal, St John's College, University of Durham

Members
The Revd Professor Michael Banner (until 1999)
F. D. Maurice Professor of Moral and Social Theology, King's College, London
Professor Richard Bauckham
Professor of New Testament Studies and Bishop Wardlaw Professor, University of St Andrews
Canon Dr Christina Baxter
Principal, St John's College, Nottingham
The Revd Dr Jeremy Begbie
Reader in Theology, Associate Director, Institute for Theology, Imagination and the Arts, University of St Andrews and Associate Principal, Ridley Hall, Cambridge
Dr Grace Davie
Reader in Sociology, University of Exeter
Professor David Ford
Regius Professor of Divinity, University of Cambridge
Professor Ann Loades
Professor of Divinity, University of Durham
Dr Alistair McFadyen
Lecturer in Theology, University of Leeds
The Revd Dr Alister McGrath (until 1998)
Principal, Wycliffe Hall, Oxford, and Professor of Historical Theology
The Right Revd Dr Geoffrey Rowell (from 1998)
Bishop of Gibraltar in Europe
The Right Revd Mark Santer (until 1999)
Retired; formerly Bishop of Birmingham
The Right Revd Dr Peter Selby
Bishop of Worcester
The Right Revd Dr Kenneth Stevenson
Bishop of Portsmouth
The Revd Canon Professor Anthony Thiselton
Professor of Theology, University of Nottingham

The Revd Dr Fraser Watts (from 1998)
Starbridge Lecturer in Science and Religion, University of Cambridge
The Revd Canon Professor John Webster
Lady Margaret Professor of Divinity, University of Oxford
Dr Linda Woodhead
Lecturer in Religious Studies, University of Lancaster

Consultant
The Revd Canon Dr Martin Kitchen (from 1999)
Canon of Durham and Vice Dean

Secretaries to the Commission
The Revd Dr Jonathan Knight (until 1998)
Director of Studies, Focus Christian Institute; formerly Chaplain and Research Assistant to the Bishop of Ely
Professor Gareth Jones (1998–99)
Professor of Christian Theology, Canterbury Christ Church University College
Dr Bridget Nichols (1999)
Lay Chaplain and Research Assistant to the Bishop of Ely
The Revd Andrew Tremlett (from 1999)
Vicar of Goring by Sea; formerly Domestic Chaplain to the Bishop of Portsmouth

Preface

This report, like its three predecessors, is published under the authority of the House of Bishops and is commended by the House to the Church for study.

On behalf of the House of Bishops
✠ Rowan Cantuar
✠ David Ebor

January 2003

Foreword

The Doctrine Commission of the General Synod of the Church of England (to give it its full title) has the task of considering and writing about matters referred to it by the House of Bishops. In the last fifteen years four reports have been published: *We Believe in God* (1987), *We Believe in the Holy Spirit* (1991), *The Mystery of Salvation* (1995) and the present book, *Being Human* (2003). In each case the text has been considered by the House of Bishops and published 'under their authority', with the commendation that it should be studied by members of the Church. The four reports are not productions of the House of Bishops, and do not therefore carry the authority which such publications would have. But neither, on the other hand, are they merely individual views of the writers. If they are not the doctrine of the Church of England, nor are they merely doctrine *in* the Church of England (to adopt the title of the famous report of the Commission in 1938).

The intention of the reports is that they should be read and received. In other words, they are part of a process of teaching and learning designed to strengthen believers in their faith and to challenge those who are uncertain about what to believe. When used and discovered to be helpful in this way they acquire an authority greater than that of formal endorsement. If on the other hand they simply sit on shelves gathering dust, they decline to the status of historical curiosity. It is simply our prayer that this text will prove to be serviceable.

In this connection we wish to record our gratitude to the Venerable Christopher Lowson, Archdeacon of Portsdown, and to the groups which he assembled to 'road-test' (as we put it) an early version of one of the chapters. We needed to hear how what we had written would be interpreted. The considerable effort which the groups expended in responding to our work was much appreciated and very instructive. We hope that the changes we introduced as a consequence have improved the text.

Like its predecessors, though rather longer in the preparation, this report is the fruit of painstaking discussion, written formulation and multiple revisions. This is not a natural process for academics, whose training encourages them to enjoy the spirited defence of their own writing, and good-tempered but inconclusive discussion. A well-conducted and satisfactory seminar is an occasion for the exchange of diverse views, not the production of an agreed text.

Yet this report is once again an agreed text, which as the Commission's Chairman I can only celebrate as the fruit of very considerable forbearance and graciousness. There are a number of particular members who were ready to act as drafters, and then as re-drafters, putting the goal of consensus ahead of their inclinations. As a previous Chairman acknowledged, we are aware of the fact that, left to ourselves, many of us would have formulated our convictions otherwise. But at the end of the day the reception of a common text has been more important to us than our personal opinions. I can honestly record the fact that, despite the known contentiousness of some of the subjects, at no stage has any member used other than argument to achieve results – and for that I am profoundly grateful.

On behalf of the Commission I should like warmly to acknowledge the help of Dr Jonathan Knight and Dr Bridget Nichols, both Research Assistants with me when I was Bishop of Ely. Dr Gareth Jones was a most able Secretary to the Commission before his appointment to a Chair of Christian Theology at Canterbury Christ Church University College. From 1999 the Commission has been marvellously served by Andrew Tremlett as Secretary; and we owe a huge debt of gratitude to Canon Dr Martin Kitchen for unfailingly efficient and constructive services as Consultant.

✠ Stephen Sykes

Chapter 1
Introduction

What is human nature?

This report is about human nature, what it means to be a person. But where to begin with that topic? Christians have had views on this subject for centuries. A book title, *Man, Fallen and Free*, summarizes in politically incorrect language a traditional view.

'What is man, that thou art mindful of him?', some of us learnt from Coverdale's translation of the Book of Psalms. The answer turns out to be a surprising affirmation of human dignity:

> When I look at your heavens, the work of your fingers,
> the moon and the stars that you have established;
> what are human beings that you are mindful of them,
> mortals that you care for them?
> Yet you have made them a little lower than God,
> and crowned them with glory and honour. (Psalm 8.3-5)

The question about human nature is not merely theoretical. All of us act on the basis of some views or assumptions about ourselves and others. How a person spends their money, conducts their intimate relationships, or develops their talents and capacities, will involve a practical resolution of the question of some kind. Power, money, sex and time are not topics we can avoid in the living of life.

There is, moreover, a vast array of new information to assimilate from the natural and social sciences, as well as formulations from philosophers of various views. We also have to take account of an argument, recently developed, that it is impossible to construct a unified theory of human nature; or rather, that all such constructs express the personal viewpoint and interests of one elite or another.

One thing is certain: that human beings do not come with instructions attached like a pack of self-assembly furniture. To be a person is evidently a project or an achievement. This is why, despite all the complexities, we want to start at a different point, with a single-sentence phrase from the Gospel of Luke, 'Jesus increased in wisdom' (Luke 2.52). That statement focuses on four key elements of this report.

First, it is about Jesus. We explore what it means to be human today, and we approach that through power, money, sex and time. Throughout, we have one human being, Jesus Christ, especially in mind. He is our primary reference point for what it means to be human in relation to God, to other people, and to creation.

Second, the statement is about wisdom. Wisdom is not the same as information or knowledge, though it includes both. Wisdom is about how we live well before God alongside other people in our world. How can we arrive at an understanding that helps to shape good living? What are the best resources for insight into basic features of human existence today? Those are wisdom questions.

Third, it is about increasing, growing, developing. Wisdom is not a destination where we or our Church can arrive at some time. It is classically described as a way, a path, or a journey. There is always more wisdom to be found, and the desire to learn it is a core dynamic in good living. In dealing with power, money, sex and time we are inviting readers to share the journey we have made together over five years and to travel further.

Fourth, the statement about Jesus is from the Bible, which is passionate in its insistence on the vital significance of wisdom. The Bible itself has been our primary written concentration of wisdom in the production of this report. We have returned to it again and again, and found it more and more generative of key insights and understandings.

This has been at the heart of our method: to bring discussion of Scripture into conversation with whatever is relevant to our topics. It has meant engaging with Christian and other wisdom from previous periods and from the present, with various academic disciplines, and with major features of our contemporary world.

The role of learning and teaching: *Homo sapiens*

Where power, money, sex and time are concerned we are all involved in them and in the desires, interests, confusions and urgencies that they bring. We are constantly making judgements and decisions about priorities for our time, how to get and spend money, how to cope with the power and consequences of sexual desire (of other people as well as our own), and how to exercise power and responsibility (whether in silence, speech, suffering or action). The quality of those judgements and decisions will depend on many factors, but a critical one is the way we perceive human life – its nature, meaning and purpose.

This is where wisdom and understanding are vital. Powerful forces converge and conflict in the spheres of power, money, sex and time – the stakes are very high. Unless these forces are understood and responded to with insight and good sense then individuals and whole families, communities, nations and regions – ultimately human life itself – are at risk. Lack of wisdom and understanding damages or destroys people, societies, and the natural ecology that sustains life.

In this situation the naming of our species *Homo sapiens*, the Latin for 'wise humanity', is worth considering. It might cynically be seen as a sad joke. But more fundamentally it points to the crucial role of human beings as learners, or not, of wisdom. To try to imagine a family, Church or nation in which there are misjudgements, wrong decisions and bad actions relating to power, money, sex and time, is to become clear how essential it is to human flourishing that we learn wisdom which can shape these four as well as other aspects of life.

This has been widely understood through human history, and all societies have had their versions of life-shaping wisdom. They have also usually paid close attention to the forms of teaching and learning which pass on wisdom and which try to develop fresh wisdom to meet new issues and situations.

Homo sapiens has another advantage as a term: its scientific use is a reminder of the important findings of various life sciences. The most dramatic instance in recent decades has been genetics and the progress it has made in understanding the human genome. This has implications for most areas of life, from personality, sex and intelligence to disease, death and free will. But it is also worth noting that it actually increases the demand for wisdom. The flood of knowledge about our genes leads to unprecedented possibilities of changing and recombining them. The most spectacular procedures, such as cloning, result in headlines, passionate debates and legislation. Other discoveries are more limited in their implications but yet increase the number of possibilities and therefore decisions. Who and what guides those decisions? In these complex issues, combining technical possibilities, judgements about what is desirable, and the assessment of effects that can last generations, how is just and wise deliberation to be achieved?

The task of learning wisdom for our situation

In most societies of the past, and some today, wisdom has been strongly traditional. It has been deeply rooted in the past, concerned to conserve the best and ensure continuity. Yet most of them have also known times of radical change during which traditional wisdom has been questioned, revised and abandoned or transformed.

The wisdom literature of Israel shows signs of the traumas the people went through. The Book of Proverbs distils from sources within and beyond Israel quite a confident understanding of how life is to be lived, with goodness rewarded and wickedness punished. The Book of Job reflects a far more traumatic experience of suffering and evil. When Job's friends turn the wisdom of Proverbs into inflexible dogma that cannot accommodate Job's experience, new questions have to be asked. The Book of Ecclesiastes raises radical questions in a very different, more personal mode. The wisdom tradition continues in books of the Apocrypha, and comes to fresh expression in the New Testament, especially in some of the teaching of Jesus, in John's Gospel, in Paul, and in the Letter of James. This is a tradition that has to cope with massive discontinuities and reorientations. There have been crises of faith, times of despair, and deep conflicts over fundamental matters.

These books offer a wisdom about wisdom. They give an example of passionately seeking wisdom before God, and that involves facing complex and often disturbing realities as truthfully as possible. Their example seems deeply appropriate to our period and civilization. Recent centuries have brought massive changes and traumas which make modernity appear very different from earlier times. It is not just that every area of life, from politics and economics to culture and leisure, has been affected. Accompanying this have been changes in consciousness, and in the way the universe, and humanity within it, are understood.

One of the most obvious features of modern life in the West has been a radical questioning of tradition, of everything received from the past. Wisdom distilled from living in previous eras has often seemed irrelevant and out of date, unsuited to modern conditions and problems. Add to all this the floods of information, images, and other stimuli that pour out from radio, television, video, compact discs, computers, the Internet, print and other media, and the result is that our attention is generally dominated by input from the present day. The quantity, intensity and novelty of all this helps to make both the past and the future seem distant and even unreal – another world. We speak of a feature of modern culture common to Europe and North America, but these regions are home to numerous people of non-western traditions who also have experienced, though in sometimes different ways, its dissenting impact. Such, moreover, is the power and reach of global communication, the same information, images and stimuli play upon and interact with very different cultural traditions.

One typical expression of it is the prominence of 'youth culture' shaped by many attitudes common in adolescence. There is a reluctance to learn from previous generations, traditions and past centuries, and an impatience with taking on responsibility for the medium- or long-term future.

Yet those same young people also go through more formal education than any generation in history. The media which inundate us with communications can, and sometimes do, facilitate access both to the past and its wisdom and to sensitive explorations of the longer-term consequences of our behaviour. One of the most important developments in modern times has been mass education, together with a huge expansion in scholarship and research. Many of the disciplines and subdisciplines are distinctively modern, especially in the natural and human sciences, and a great deal of education is in the know-how and skills needed by the modern market economy. Other areas of study are in more continuity with pre-modern disciplines – history, languages, literature, philosophy, mathematics, music, theology, and so on.

That would in fact need to be qualified a good deal to take account of what acquiring of wisdom actually goes on in all sorts of formal and informal ways. Young people learn a good deal from intensive engagement with their peers; and as pupils or students they learn from their studies and their teachers, and by developing know-how and skills. For people of all ages, wisdom enters into their deliberations, judgements and decisions. The pressures of life constantly lead to a search for wisdom, even if it is usually named other things – a better perspective, standing back from things, taking everything into account, thinking about something from various people's standpoints, considering values as well as facts, mentoring, counselling, therapy, having an integrated personality, taking an ethical approach, evaluating, practising a spirituality, consulting an 'agony aunt', and so on.

So there is plenty of wisdom-seeking by individuals – and there are similar searches by groups and organizations. The large market for management philosophies and techniques shows the desire to shape organizations better. Yet it is hard to see wisdom-seeking as a strong feature in our culture. At the very least we need to make it a more conscious desire and aim. The pursuit of information, knowledge and know-how has terrible potential if not accompanied by wisdom. Some of the nastiest shocks of modernity have come from technologies being used to carry out genocide, unprecedentedly destructive wars, or environmental devastation. These have been backed up by modern education, communications, economics, bureaucracy, management expertise and science.

The cry for wisdom is a desire for ways of human flourishing in the face of problems caused mainly by human agency; it is also, more basically, a cry for survival. Those sensational disasters are just the tip of an iceberg. Many traditions converge in naming the basic problem as lack of wisdom.

So if there is discontinuity with wisdom traditions of the past, if our culture and education fail to make wisdom a high enough priority, and if there is a crying need for it in coping with extreme dangers as well as in seeking the ordinary well-being of individuals and societies, what should we be aiming at?

Our way forward

We see the way forward in a combination of elements. We need to draw on the wisdom of previous generations, including those who had to face the inadequacies of the wisdom they inherited without abandoning what was of continuing value. We need to learn from the experiences and wisdom of modern life. In the light of all that, we need to engage as thoroughly as possible with the places of vitality and suffering in our world. The aim is for the often terrible wounds and pathologies to receive healing, to try to cope with our world's traumas and problems, and to serve the flourishing of humanity and the rest of creation. This can be summed up as wisdom in the service of the common good.

That is the general answer. But it is also therefore very vague. Many religions, philosophies, ideologies and spiritualities would agree on such an aim but differ deeply in how to try to achieve it. The thirst is for particular answers. That is why we are engaging mainly with power, money, sex and time, four specific areas of life which test all available wisdom. But our teaching on those four is in the context of a larger particularity: the Anglican way of Christian faith in Jesus Christ. That is the specific 'ecology' in which our thinking is done.

To look to a particular community and tradition that has a good deal of historical experience is to recognize that in matters requiring wisdom there can be no fresh start. We cannot unthink or undo our inheritance from the past any more than we can disown the four billion or so years that have gone into developing our genes. It is that heritage, genetic and historical, which gives us the capacities, understanding and communities through which to cope with living and deciding now. But why the Anglican way?

Anglicanism: a wisdom tradition for the twenty-first century

As Anglican Christians our core identity is as followers of Jesus Christ along with many others, seeking to participate in the love of God for the whole of creation and in God's wisdom for ourselves and others. The most obvious features of Anglicanism as a wisdom tradition are those it shares with many other parts of the Christian community. It is nourished by the Bible and its wisdom, which is inseparable from other dimensions such as worship, doctrine, law, history and prophecy. Continuity with the Early Church is valued highly. Its struggle to discern the best ways to shape its life, worship and teaching was closely bound up with engagement with its Jewish roots and its pagan context, including a sophisticated Hellenistic and Roman culture that had its own wisdom traditions. One way of describing that struggle is as a quest for a characteristic Christian wisdom.

The continually renewed appeal to sources in the first millennium of Christianity is not an uncritical repetition of them in changed circumstances. Rather, it is an attempt to draw on the wisdom and truth that were distilled from those centuries of worship, discipleship, suffering, study, and often conflictual deliberation. Unless later Christians in their situations show a comparable intensity, imagination and faithfulness as worshippers, disciples, sufferers, learners and debaters of truth and practice, then they are not sustaining the same tradition. As basic features of early Christianity are taken up with wisdom in modern situations their fruitfulness is repeatedly experienced. This can be seen in matters as varied as uniting the Old with the New Testament in the canon of Scripture, patterns of eucharistic worship, engagement with philosophy and other aspects of a culture, forms of Church order, and the significance of monastic patterns of life such as the Benedictine and Augustinian.

The tragic divisions of the Church which began in the early centuries increased dramatically in the second millennium, beginning with the schism between the Eastern and Western Churches in 1054. That split and the even greater upheaval of the sixteenth-century Protestant Reformation have not been regarded by Anglicans as a case of the 'true Church' splitting off from those who were not truly fellow Christians. Both splits were terrible wounds to the Church as the body of Christ, and they left all sides impaired. The imperative now is for wise healing.

Anglicanism's distinctiveness as a Church is partly shaped through its Reformation history. That is worth noting well, because it can be seen to be of continuing and even increasing importance in the twenty-first century. There are some similarities globally today with Europe in the Reformation period: massive changes in many areas, new media and economic forces, and religious conflicts threatening the whole fabric of civilization. The Reformation was simultaneously a release of new life and a founding trauma of the modern period. It combined a fresh vitality of Christian faith with deadly conflicts which discredited religion. Anglicanism has been an attempt to live from the vitality at the same time as facing conflicts and fostering the common good.

Learning from this history is as important as ever. The combination of ways in which Anglicanism has responded to modern problems and possibilities means that it is a Christian wisdom tradition that offers a home (with the imperfections of any family life), nourishment, and a way of life for the twenty-first century. It has maintained worship and learning from Scripture as central to Christian life. There has been a strong commitment to education and its institutions, and to mature, intelligent discipleship in all spheres. Findings in scholarship and the sciences have been taken seriously and thought through in relation to Christian faith. Pastoral and political ethics have been tested and refined in many settings. Staying close to localities in their particularity has continued to be a priority. In Church organization it has tried to avoid not only authoritarianism but also sectarian forms of freedom that encourage fragmentation. Instead, through historical struggle and negotiation (a process which continues and is in an important phase at present) a form of Church order has evolved, the aim of which is a global communion with continuity in order and mutual accountability. Essential to that are forms of consultation and deliberation which may seem to some traditions to be too messy and public, allowing for conflicts between positions and parties that can be unedifying. This high cost of seeking a common mind is in the service of a mission which at its best combines evangelism, chaplaincy to many institutions and groups, and widely distributed responsibility for faithful life and witness.

The challenge to us as a Doctrine Commission has been to listen to various sources of wisdom on power, money, sex and time, and to try to work out through that engagement what it means to be human beings before God now in the twenty-first century.

What we hope to teach

So we are first of all learners and teachers. What do we hope readers of this report might receive? It is worth summarizing what we are offering in relation to each of the four topics. It will be noted that much of what is being offered is not in the form of neat answers to problems. Learning wisdom is often a matter of learning how to live in hope, faith and love with many problems unsolved. Questions sometimes need to be deepened and broadened, with the wisest answers often opening up further questions. Yet there can still be an appropriate definiteness in teaching, and confidence in putting it forward as a tested, durable resource for living well.

On power we want to say that the God who gives us life, the 'God of power and might', draws us into a surprising and adventurous refashioning of what it might mean for us to exercise God-given powers of body, mind and spirit. We are not left at the mercy of what the concept of power has become in western thought – an ominous, looming and predominantly negative idea. Though we have good reason to learn from the history of how power has been abused, by Church people as well as by sovereigns, dictators and political leaders, suspicion is not the whole story. There is a way in which we can exercise the powers we have and acquire, both in service to others and self-critically.

On money we want to raise alertness to Jesus' teaching that it is impossible to serve God and Mammon, specifically in the context of what money has become in the modern world. When a human invention with many positive features becomes a mostly invisible controlling force in our lives, then it is time for the wise to take notice. There are both spiritual and practical habits to be acquired if money is to occupy a disciplined place in our lives. Being human before God involves learning the grace of generosity both with who we are and what we own. There is such a thing, we believe, as money-discipleship. That is a discipline not easily achieved. We need the help of a community in which to learn from good examples, to profit from constructive criticism and to experience generosity of forgiveness for acknowledged failure.

On sex the basic thing to be learnt is that it is created to be 'a whole-person relationship of love and loyalty involving body and self'. We teach a realism about the goodness and joy of sex together with the ways it can go terribly wrong. This is set in the context of God's engagement with the world, and especially the encompassing reality of that engagement: the covenant relationship with God, other people and creation. The last word is neither the created goodness nor the wrongness but the reality and offer of transformation, as sex is taken up into renewed covenant relationships, the desire for the kingdom of God is made primary, virtues such as faithfulness, patience and gratitude are learnt, and the various sexual developments in our culture are tested for their wisdom or foolishness.

On time, apparently the most abstract and difficult of our topics, we want to draw attention to the radicality of the project of living in and with time as a good gift of God to us as creatures. Time is not a divinity, nor on the other hand is it the realm of fallenness and futility. It is within this life that we taste and enjoy through the Holy Spirit the second gift of time redeemed by Jesus Christ. This should transform our understanding of the significance of worship. Far from being a 'spare time' activity, in a life dominated by clocks, worship opens us out onto the 'time of our lives', creating and nurturing habits of life in attentiveness and joy. There is here, we believe, a wisdom to be absorbed by means of what we call 'the temporal virtues': patience and faithfulness, forgiveness and gratitude, alertness and rest, repentance and hope, and wisdom and improvisation.

In tackling these specific subjects we are also trying to commend an approach to being human which is more widely relevant. It is apparent to us that serious ethical and legal problems now confront human beings as a result of advances in genetics and neurology. A Christian response to these issues would be simple if it were a matter of consulting a moral code, and pronouncing a development to be right or wrong. Of course one would still have to consider the question of whether such a code would be equally authoritative for all people, irrespective of their religious beliefs or lack of them. This is the idea of a 'natural' moral law, which (it is claimed) resides in the hearts and minds of all. But even if there were such a code, and that is disputed, the difficulty would remain. For the fact is that the scientific advances are not foreseen as possibilities in Scripture or in the traditions which subsequently developed on the basis of Scripture. Indeed even modern regulatory codes struggle to catch up with what science is making possible.

This, however, is only one aspect of the difficulty. If – as seems entirely conceivable – what can be carried out by way of genetic or neurological manipulation results in an alteration to a human being, the question immediately arises whether such an altered (?enhanced) being would be 'human' as we understand that word. On the face of it, we would be able to answer that question if we were able to say for certain what a human being was, what was consistent with 'human nature'. Again, a Christian response to these issues would be simple if it were a matter of consulting authoritative teaching on human nature (what has been called 'theological anthropology'), and pronouncing the development to be consistent or inconsistent with it. But as soon as one immerses oneself in the content of that sub-discipline of theology one discovers oneself in great thickets of traditional disputes, about, for example, 'the Fall' and 'original sin', which apparently bear little direct relation to the urgent questions under consideration. The plain fact is that what is now possible or at least thinkable was not possible at the time at which these traditional doctrines were being developed. The basic datum which all the traditions of theological anthropology presupposed was that being conceived was a kind of lottery, the results of which one simply had to accept. But it is that 'given' which has been taken away. The question now is, is there any reason why we should not improve on the results of the accidents of conception?

A Christian response to this may well have two parts to it. In the first place it is true that the traditional content of Christian teaching about human nature contains direct implications for certain kinds of unacceptable manipulations. Human beings are understood as bearing moral responsibility for their actions before God. To make a person subject to the will of another, by the involuntary administration of drugs or an implant in the brain, would be to deny that person the possibility of moral responsibility. Such a 'development' would be unhesitatingly condemned. That something similar occurs in the treatment of hyperactive children or persons suffering from certain mental illnesses rightly gives rise to concerns. We are quite properly anxious to preserve for human beings the possibility of making their own decisions and moral choices. This is a reasonable implication of Christian teaching about human nature, and one, moreover, which commends itself to many people who do not share Christian faith.

But a second response is also possible from Christians. That is, that none of these topics could be reliably tackled without the development of the wisdom of which we have spoken. It is not a matter of looking up the solution to a problem in some kind of text book, and citing it as a final answer. It is, rather, the discipline of thinking an issue through, trying to understand as many of its implications as possible, both for the individuals closely concerned and also for society as a whole. The wisdom to judge rightly in such complex matters is not easily won, and is likely to involve argument between people of different convictions. It certainly involves a capacity to understand the pressures by which we are surrounded, the hidden factors which predispose us to respond in certain ways and which shape our self-understanding.

This report is mostly about human nature in that sense, a 'being human' at this particular time in history, a practical task of contemporary discipleship demanding of us great wisdom. We have written about power, money, sex and time, both because nobody can be a human being today without developing a wise way of understanding and coping with these realities, and because of the wider implications which wisdom in those areas might have for other aspects of human being in this new time. We urgently need to 'increase in wisdom'.

Chapter 2
Listening to Scripture

Wisdom is not primarily about accepting certain conclusions. It is about the habits of individuals and communities. These habits of mind, heart, imagination and will can help us, in the ever-changing circumstances of our lives, to find a wisdom that is in line with the purposes of God.

There are many elements in forming such habits. Becoming gripped by the desire for wisdom, and learning how to fulfil the desire, usually happens through family, friends, teachers and groups. This face-to-face scale in the communication of wisdom is something that needs sustaining and developing – a good deal of the communication of information and knowledge can do without it, but wisdom cannot. It is not so much about transferring data and conclusions, but is more like an apprenticeship in ways of learning, relating, deliberating, judging and deciding. Such apprenticeships are of the utmost importance to families, churches, schools and other places of learning.

Within the Christian Church there is one unique authoritative expression of teaching which has arisen out of centuries of face-to-face transmission of the faith, first in Israel and later in Christianity. This is the Bible. Down the centuries Christian teaching has been characterized by intensive listening to and conversation around the Bible and around the issues of life in the context of prayer, worship and attending to others (past and present). The wisdom that the Spirit gives is nourished by Scripture understood through tradition and reason. In the course of time this leads to the development of teaching into doctrines and theologies.

So the 'how' of learning wisdom has to have at its heart the interpretation of Scripture, leading through commentary and discussion to teaching. As a Commission we have increasingly converged on this, and have engaged in biblical interpretation together. One outcome is that each chapter draws on Scripture, and we also include a few of the interpretations of specific passages which we have produced to help our deliberations. In addition we recommend in this chapter two sets of biblical texts for special study in relation to the report as a whole, and we do some introductory commentary on them. We then offer a distillation of what we find most important in the tradition of Christian doctrine on the subject of being human.

Biblical wisdom

We have selected two sets of biblical texts through which to open up the themes of power, money, sex and time. The concern will not be detailed commentary so much as finding an orientation for being human before God. We encourage readers to meditate on these texts as an appropriate way into the rest of the report.

First, there are the Old Testament wisdom books of Proverbs, Ecclesiastes and the Song of Songs. Second, there are the two New Testament writings of Luke, his Gospel and the Acts of the Apostles. But before turning to them we pause to note the importance of the third regular liturgical element from Scripture, the Psalms. Their daily use shapes life through primary orientation towards God in worship. Their realism about the full range of human experience ensures that there is no escapism. And their intersection with the wisdom traditions intensifies the most basic wisdom maxim:

> The fear of the Lord is the beginning of wisdom;
> All those who practise it have a good understanding.
> His praise endures for ever. (Psalm 111.10)

Biblical wisdom is intrinsically connected with worship in awe and reverence, and living life in awareness that we are always before God and accountable to God. John Donne calls the fear of the Lord

> the art of arts, the root, and fruit, of all true wisdom ... As he that is fallen into the king's hand for debt to him, is safe from all other creditors, so is he, that fears the Lord, from other fears. He that loves the Lord, loves him with all his love; he that fears the Lord, loves him with all his fear too; God takes no half affections.

So in considering power, money, sex and time our first and most basic practical teaching is: join in a regular worshipping community. There will be found the wisest way of shaping life in the world, by praising and thanking God, confessing sin, receiving forgiveness, learning from Scripture, praying for others, participating in Jesus Christ, and being sent to take part in fulfilling God's purposes in the world.

Proverbs, Ecclesiastes and the Song of Songs

But stop for a moment and think: how many people do you know whom you would describe as wise? How many people can you say, without qualification, live their lives day by day, even moment by moment, in a way that honours and glorifies God? For that is what 'wisdom' meant to the biblical writers: living in the world in such a way that God, and God's intentions for the world, are acknowledged in all we do. It sounds like a lofty goal, perhaps too lofty for ordinary people living busy lives. Such a goal of wisdom seems attainable only for great saints; maybe a hermit or a monastic could achieve it. Yet this is not the understanding of the biblical writers. It is important to recognise at the outset that they consider wisdom within the grasp of every person who desires it wholeheartedly. Wisdom does not require any special intellectual gifts. The fruit of wisdom, a well-ordered life and a peaceful mind, results not from high IQ but from a disposition of the heart that the sages (wisdom teachers) of Israel most often call 'fear of the Lord'.

Ellen Davis, whose commentary on the three books is itself a work of considerable wisdom, and from whose work the above quotation comes, sees them as 'spiritual guidance for ordinary people' and largely produced by ordinary people. This wisdom is located at the centre of daily life that desires to love God with all the mind as well as heart and strength.

Proverbs, Ecclesiastes and the Song of Songs are carefully composed poetry, distilling centuries of wisdom, and drawing on other traditions (especially Egyptian) as well as their own. They are meant to be read slowly, and meditated upon, ideally learnt by heart. They are a reliable way to form a truthful moral imagination and so an ideal preparation for considering the topics of this report. It is all the more advisable to study them because they are not well covered in most Christian lectionaries and courses of Bible study. Yet they have, with good reason, been among the favourite books of many rabbis of Israel and teachers of the Church.

Proverbs is passionate about the learning of wisdom, which unites obedience to God with wide-ranging knowledge of the human and natural world:

> She is more precious than jewels,
> And nothing you desire can compare with her. (Proverbs 3.15)

Proverbs is also devastating on the consequences of not learning wisdom: death, destruction, social disintegration, political and ecological disaster, lives and reputations ruined, stumbling, panic, misery, evil of all sorts.

The basic conviction is clear:

> The Lord by wisdom founded the earth;
> by understanding he established the heavens. (Proverbs 3.19)

Creation is the work of wisdom, and so we need wisdom if our world is to be inhabited and cared for well. This wisdom is not only utterly self-involving as the goal of our leading desire; it is also simultaneously others-involving, God-involving and world-involving. These fundamental features of wisdom are no different today, and challenge Christian teaching to be comparably lively and multifaceted.

Ecclesiastes takes a very different approach to wisdom from that of Proverbs. The fear of God is equally fundamental, but the treatment of the author's favourite themes of wisdom, pleasure, work, money and power is daringly different from the rest of the Bible. He is by turns earthy, scathingly critical, agnostic, sceptical, disillusioned, despairing, pleasure-loving, irreligious, contradictory, pessimistic and even cynical. He illustrates well that the Bible offers no smoothly integrated systematic theology. Indeed, the wisdom literature as a whole, where Ecclesiastes and Job can question much that is found in Proverbs and elsewhere, is a strong invitation into wrestling with issues that are bound to remain unfathomed and unresolved. The answers are not given in advance of entering the depths, including facing doubt and despair. In Christian terms this anguish of wrestling with reality at its darkest points hints at the culmination of wisdom seen in the crucifixion of Jesus Christ.

Before the modern period the Song of Songs generated a huge amount of Christian and Jewish commentary. In the formative period of rabbinic Judaism Rabbi Akiba's verdict was: 'All the Scriptures are holy, but the Song of Songs is the Holy of Holies.' It has led generations of Jews and Christians into the heart of those basic relationships where things can go most wonderfully right or most terribly wrong: between man and woman, humanity and the earth, and humanity and God.

The Song's passionate intimacy sensitively testifies to the joys and agonies of love. It is also jewelled with references, direct and more subtle, to other parts of Scripture. The effect on the reader who traces these connections is to be drawn into several levels of meaning. There is the mutual love and ecstasy of the lovers. There is also celebration of the natural world:

> The flowers appear on the earth;
> the time of singing has come,
> and the voice of the turtle-dove is heard in our land.
> The fig tree puts forth its figs,
> and the vines are in blossom;
> they give forth their fragrance ... (Song of Songs 2.12-13)

15

The beauty and fruitfulness of the land of Israel are savoured, and this is concentrated in the joy of a garden. Delight in the land and the paradise of a garden has many biblical resonances, and these multiply as other echoes are recognized. By the end we have been led through the creation stories of Genesis, the Exodus wilderness, the anguished love relationship between God and Israel (especially recalling the poetry in Hosea and Isaiah), the decorative symbols of the Temple (pomegranates, lions, lilies, palm trees) as well as the worship and feasting that took place there, and the significance of the city of Jerusalem. And again and again the language of the lovers calls to mind the greatest commandment of all, to 'love the Lord your God with all your heart, and with all your soul, and with all your might' (Deuteronomy 6.5).

It is also worth noting that in the Septuagint, the Greek translation of the Scriptures which was the Bible of the New Testament writers, the word for 'love' in the Song is *agape* (as celebrated by Paul in 1 Corinthians 13):

> ... for love is strong as death ...

> Many waters cannot quench love,
> neither can floods drown it.
> If one offered for love
> all the wealth of one's house,
> it would be utterly scorned. (Song of Songs 8.6-7)

The Gospel of Luke and the Acts of the Apostles

The Gospel of Luke together with the Acts of the Apostles summarize what came to be accepted in the Church as the framework for understanding the origins of Christianity. Luke insists on strong continuity with the Old Testament (which was, of course, his only Bible), and in that context tells the story of Jesus from his birth through baptism, temptation, ministry, transfiguration, Last Supper, passion, death, resurrection and ascension. Then, with equal emphasis on the Old Testament, he tells the story of the Early Church from the ascension of Jesus and the coming of the Holy Spirit at Pentecost in Jerusalem until Paul's two years as a prisoner in Rome.

For our purposes Luke's writings are especially helpful for their teaching on power and money. They do not have much on sex in a narrow sense, but much on love and other closely related matters. They have also been extraordinarily influential in shaping the Christian understanding of time, as will appear below. But above all they offer a distinctive Christian wisdom centred on Jesus Christ. The statement towards the beginning of the Gospel, 'Jesus increased in wisdom'

(Luke 2.52), is given its richest meaning in the last chapter. There the resurrected Jesus teaches his disciples through Scripture.

One statement is so important that it is repeated three times with variations in the one chapter. This key to interpretation is that Jesus of Nazareth, 'a prophet mighty in deed and word before God and all the people' (Luke 24.19) was crucified and raised (Luke 24.19-25, 25-27, 46). So the culmination of his wisdom is interpreting the Scriptures seeing those events as the realization of the purposes of God in history. The life, death and resurrection of Jesus are therefore at the heart of Christian identity in the gospel, in baptism, in the creeds, in Holy Communion, and in the Christian Year. Christian wisdom is also centred in this person who is incarnate, crucified and risen.

In the life of Jesus the goodness of creation and human life is radically affirmed. Jesus' teaching of the kingdom of God invites everyone into an unimaginable abundance of life. His actions give vivid signs of the reality of this – forgiving, healing, exorcising, feeding, partying, storytelling, blessing. In his crucifixion Jesus suffers and exposes the grim reality of sin and death. It is a judgement on what is wrong with human life, while at the same time denying that they have the last word: 'Father, forgive them, for they do not know what they are doing'; '... today you will be with me in Paradise'; 'Father, into your hands I commend my spirit' (Luke 23.34, 43, 46). In his resurrection the dead Jesus is transformed, raised to new life which can be shared without limitation. He inspires joy (Luke 24.41, 52), and sends the Holy Spirit as the energizer and guide of transformed living and communication 'in his name' (Luke 24.47).

That threefold reality of the incarnate, crucified and risen Jesus, who affirms, judges and transforms the world and human life, is the most condensed expression of Christian wisdom. This report tries to treat power, money, sex and time with that Christ-centred realism: each of them is to be affirmed, judged and transformed. Damaging distortions happen when understanding and behaviour are shaped by only one or only two of those equally vital activities.

In Luke this teaching involves intense frustration: 'Oh, how foolish you are, and how slow of heart to believe ...' (Luke 24.25). But there is hope for teachers too: 'Were not our hearts burning within us while he was talking to us on the road, while he was opening the scriptures to us?' (Luke 24.32).

The short meditations which follow are intended both to encourage further meditation and to open up the topics of later chapters.

Power

> Whoever sows injustice will reap calamity;
> and the rod of anger will fail. (Proverbs 22.8)
>
> Wise warriors are mightier than strong ones,
> and those who have knowledge than those who have strength.
> (Proverbs 24.5)
>
> By justice a king gives stability to the land,
> but one who makes heavy exactions ruins it. (Proverbs 29.4)
>
> If a king judges the poor with equity,
> his throne will be established for ever. (Proverbs 29.14)

Such statements which affirm a God-given and God-supported moral
order could be multiplied many times. They need to be faced with
statements of doubt and disillusionment, as by Ecclesiastes:

> Again, I considered all the oppressions that are practised under the
> sun. Look, the tears of the oppressed – with no one to comfort them!
> On the side of their oppressors there was power – with no one to
> comfort them. And I thought the dead, who have already died, more
> fortunate than the living … (Ecclesiastes 4.1-2)

Yet for all the open-eyed realism about the misuse of power and
discouragement because of a lack of obvious divine retribution, the Old
Testament (including Ecclesiastes: cf. 12.13-14) is overwhelming in its
trust that the basic and encompassing truth about power is the power
of God. That is power united with wisdom, justice and compassion.

It is a fundamental issue for any society or civilization whether it
acknowledges such a moral order. The Old Testament shows it being
learnt the hard way by Israel through its turbulent history in which long
periods seemed to disconfirm it. Any wisdom about power that wants to
be faithful to that tradition needs to be comparably persistent in seeking
God and the truth of history together. Luke's two works are in deep
continuity with this. John the Baptist's radical judgement on his
generation as 'You brood of vipers' (Luke 3.7) is based on classic biblical
principles of justice in the exercise of power:

> Even tax collectors came to be baptized, and they asked him,
> 'Teacher, what should we do?' In reply he said to them, 'Collect no
> more than the amount prescribed for you.' Soldiers also asked him,
> 'And we, what should we do?' He said to them, 'Do not extort

money from anyone by threats or false accusation, and be satisfied with your wages.' (Luke 3.12-14)

Throughout Luke's Gospel and Acts an Old Testament understanding of how power serves the purposes of God in history is maintained. The political context of Jesus and of the Early Church is carefully noted, and the very last phrase of Acts underlines the importance of this, with Paul in Rome 'proclaiming the kingdom of God ... with all boldness and without hindrance' (Acts 28.31). Acts initiates a long history of confrontation, negotiation and collaboration between Christians and those in power.

In both Old and New Testaments the setting for all this is the ultimate vision of what Jesus called the kingdom of God. One focus for meditation on this in Luke is Jesus' teaching on power in the kingdom of God, anticipated by his mother's Magnificat:

> He has brought down the powerful from their thrones,
> and lifted up the lowly. (Luke 1.52)

The most extended expression of this reversal in Luke is the sermon by Jesus in Luke 6.20-49, sometimes called the Sermon on the Plain. The most explicit and radical challenge to the usual practices of power is his repeated teaching on who is the greatest, culminating at the Last Supper:

> The kings of the Gentiles lord it over them; and those in authority are called benefactors. But not so with you; rather the greatest among you must become like the youngest, and the leader like one who serves ... I am among you as one who serves. (Luke 22.25-27)

That final statement about himself goes to the heart of the Christian concept of power: it is embodied in Jesus. Luke is clear about this from the start:

> ... and you will name him Jesus. He will be great, and will be called the Son of the Most High, and the Lord God will give to him the throne of his ancestor David. He will reign over the house of Jacob for ever, and of his kingdom there will be no end. (Luke 1.31-33)

The task all this sets for the Christian understanding of power is how we can do justice both to the ultimacy of Jesus Christ and also to the need to interpret him and his teaching in new situations, learning from both the Bible and tradition.

Money

> Two things I ask of you;
> do not deny them to me before I die:
> Remove far from me falsehood and lying;
> give me neither poverty nor riches;
> feed me with the food that I need,
> or I shall be full, and deny you,
> and say, 'Who is the Lord?'
> or I shall be poor, and steal,
> and profane the name of my God. (Proverbs 30.7-9)

Proverbs is full of sensible advice about wealth and poverty. It teaches the wisdom of 'enough', and virtues such as steady work, honesty, prudence and generosity. There is spiritual risk in having more than enough or less than enough. In both, the main danger is of betraying the first principle of wisdom, the fear of the Lord. More positively, money is relativized by the superior value of wisdom – 'better than silver', 'better than gold', 'more precious than jewels', 'nothing you desire can compare with her' (3.14-15). That wisdom combines responsible ways to support oneself and to sustain a long-term economy with the imperative of concern for the poor:

> If you close your ear to the cry of the poor,
> you will cry out and not be heard. (Proverbs 21.13)

This taking up of money into an economy of desire and wisdom relating to both God and concern for the poor is again in continuity with what is found in Luke's Gospel and Acts. The wisdom there is summed up in the priority of the kingdom of God. In the course of teaching about the dangers of greed and storing up treasures, the foolishness of anxiety about possessions, and the desirability of generosity in almsgiving, the core theological wisdom is:

> For it is the nations of the world that strive after all these things, and your Father knows that you need them. Instead, strive for his kingdom, and these things will be given to you as well.
> (Luke 12.30-31)

As with power, the kingdom of God's vision of an economy of generosity raises a basic question about the character of God and the universe. Do we trust a wisdom that relies on God and a merciful economy? The Sermon on the Plain describes two economies. There are the surprising exchanges, mercy and generosity of Luke 6.27-30:

But I say to you that listen, Love your enemies, do good to those
who hate you, bless those who curse you, pray for those who abuse
you. If anyone strikes you on the cheek, offer the other also; and
from anyone who takes away your coat do not withhold even your
shirt. Give to everyone who begs from you; and if anyone takes away
your goods, do not ask for them again.

Then there are the unsurprising, self-interested exchanges in the
economy of calculation and equivalence which is worldly wisdom:

If you love those who love you, what credit is that to you? For even
sinners love those who love them. If you do good to those who do
good to you, what credit is that to you? For even sinners do the
same. If you lend to those from whom you hope to receive, what
credit is that to you? Even sinners lend to sinners, to receive as much
again. (Luke 6.32-34)

The gospel is about the reality of the economy of generosity, which
shares the character of God – compassionate, kind, merciful – and it
offers resources for being like God in this. Jesus summed up the
fundamental alternatives: 'You cannot serve God and wealth
(Mammon)' (Luke 16.13). Yet that saying comes soon after the parable
of the unjust steward and its lesson:

And his master commended the dishonest manager because he had
acted shrewdly; for the children of this age are more shrewd in
dealing with their own generation than are the children of light. And
I tell you, make friends for yourselves by means of dishonest wealth
so that when it is gone, they may welcome you into the eternal
homes. (Luke 16.8-9)

Both economies use money; there is no superior purity in trying to have
nothing to do with money; and the kingdom of God can gain from
shrewdness and from learning 'the ways of the world'. As with the
ambiguities of power, this realism about money requires continual
discernment and learning from Christians and others who have wrestled
with the issues.

Sex

Realism about sex is a mark of Proverbs. There is a grim realism about
its power to mislead and to wreck lives (5.1-14; 7.1-21). There is also a
passionate affirmation of its goodness and delights (usually from a man's
viewpoint):

> Let your fountain be blessed,
> and rejoice in the wife of your youth,
> a lovely deer, a graceful doe.
> May her breasts satisfy you at all times;
> may you be intoxicated always by her love.
> (Proverbs 5.18-19)

The culmination is in Proverbs 31.10-31, a portrayal of the dignity, understanding and social power of a woman that is unparalleled in the ancient world (significantly from a woman's viewpoint, that of Lemuel's mother). This 'valorous woman' lives out her understanding in all areas of life, including that of a mature, faithful marriage, and she also passes on her wisdom:

> She opens her mouth with wisdom,
> and the teaching of kindness is on her tongue.
> (Proverbs 31.26)

This is just what Ecclesiastes seems to mourn the lack of in his own life: 'One man among a thousand I found, but a woman among all these I have not found' (Ecclesiastes 7.28). His loneliness, filled with intense disappointment, testifies to the importance of the relationships he does not have.

Those three classic images of sex – unwise, wise, and disappointed – are joined by the Song of Songs. Proverbs sets the delights of sex in the context of a full life lived with and for others in marriage and multiple responsibilities; the Song (as introduced above) gives a more vivid, ecstatic evocation of the delights, and its imagery interweaves and enriches them with delight in gardens, the land and its seasons, the Temple, and God. At its heart is full mutuality between the man and the woman. There is no subordination of one to the other, but a passionate, loving intimacy which is fed by mutual respect and praise:

> As an apple tree among the trees of the wood,
> so is my beloved among young men.
> With great delight I sat in his shadow,
> and his fruit was sweet to my taste.
> He brought me to the banqueting house,
> and his intention toward me was love.
> Sustain me with raisins,
> refresh me with apples;
> for I am faint with love.
> O that his left hand were under my head,
> and that his right hand embraced me! (Song of Songs 2.3-6)

> You have ravished my heart, my sister, my bride,
> you have ravished my heart with a glance of your eyes,
> with one jewel of your necklace.
> How sweet is your love, my sister, my bride!
> How much better is your love than wine,
> and the fragrance of your oils than any spice!
> Your lips distil nectar, my bride;
> honey and milk are under your tongue;
> the scent of your garments is like the scent of Lebanon.
> (Song of Songs 4.9-11)

There is a realism too, in the experience of the agonies of love. But the core reality is unshaken:

> I am my beloved's and my beloved is mine. (Song of Songs 6.3)

And the urgent listening and hastening of the final exchange points to the uncertainty, the unfulfilled desire and the anticipation that are experienced by lovers of God as well as between human lovers:

> (Man)
> O you who dwell in the gardens,
> my companions are listening for your voice;
> let me hear it.
>
> (Woman)
> Make haste, my beloved,
> and be like a gazelle
> or a young stag
> upon the mountains of spices! (Song of Songs 8.13-14)

In what they say related to sex, Luke's Gospel and Acts focus on gender, male/female role divisions and championing the vulnerable. There is also a relativizing of family in relation to the kingdom of God:

> ... a woman in the crowd raised her voice and said to him, 'Blessed is the womb that bore you and the breasts that nursed you!' But he said, 'blessed rather are those who hear the word of God and obey it'. (Luke 11.27-28; cf. 8.20-21)

That is followed by a passage in which Jesus speaks of himself as a prophet 'greater than Jonah' and also as 'greater than Solomon'. In relation to our chosen Old Testament texts, all of which were ascribed to Solomon, this is a specially fruitful focus for meditation:

> The queen of the South will rise at the judgment with the people of this generation and condemn them, because she came from the ends of the earth to listen to the wisdom of Solomon, and see, something greater than Solomon is here! (Luke 11.31)

That is both an affirmation of listening to Solomon and his wisdom tradition, and also an urgent warning to listen even more attentively to the wisdom of Jesus. But it is more than that: the emphasis is not only on what Jesus says but on his person. What might it mean to be someone 'greater than Solomon'? In Luke 11.27-32 Jesus is identified as closely as possible with the word of God and the wisdom of God. The Christian wisdom tradition, in relation to sex and the other topics, is an exploration of what that means in each generation. In Luke, as in the other Gospels and the Old Testament, the fundamental guidance is to love God and one's neighbour (Luke 10.27), and that basic commandment of *agape*, as we have seen above (p. 16), is tied into the passionate *agape* of the Song of Songs.

Time

Understanding for life, education in the fullest sense, is the main concern of Proverbs and Ecclesiastes, and that demands time for slow learning and learning wisdom about time. It is wisdom across the age gap, distilled from the previous generations of many peoples, and now being passed on.

Proverbs finds stability and continuity with the past through the lives of those who have lived wisely and well:

> ... the root of the righteous will never be moved. (Proverbs 12.3)

> ... the house of the righteous will stand. (Proverbs 12.7)

Similarly, there is confidence in God's future:

> The hope of the righteous ends in gladness ... (Proverbs 10.28)

> The righteous will never be removed ... (Proverbs 10.30)

> ... the root of the righteous bears fruit (Proverbs 12.12)

Good time is shaped through living well before God. Wisdom takes the long view both backwards and forwards, building into the present a lively, respectful relationship to previous and future generations, including the honouring of parents (cf. 30.11). This includes teaching about temporal virtues such as prudence, patience, control of impulsive speaking, faithfulness, and hope. Ecclesiastes radically questions this understanding of history on the basis of what he observes happening:

> The people of long ago are not remembered,
> nor will there be any remembrance
> of people yet to come
> by those who come after them. (Ecclesiastes 1.11)

He questions the whole wisdom project:

> I applied my mind to know wisdom and to know madness and folly. I perceived that this also is but chasing after wind. For in much wisdom is much vexation, and those who increase knowledge increase sorrow. (Ecclesiastes 1.17-18)

Most radically, death and the 'vanity' of things that pass away make all desires and activities pointless:

> How can the wise die just like fools? So I hated life, because what is done under the sun was grievous to me; for all is vanity and a chasing after wind. (Ecclesiastes 2.16-17)

Yet that is not his last word, and his disillusionment with endless work leads to a breakthrough into recognizing the preciousness of what God gives in the present:

> There is nothing better for mortals than to eat and drink, and find enjoyment in their toil. This also, I saw, is from the hand of God; for apart from him who can eat or who can have enjoyment? (Ecclesiastes 2.24)

The theme of time runs through all that Ecclesiastes writes. His key term, *hevel*, means literally 'mist, vapour, breath', and signifies the fleetingness of earthly reality. It is unstable, ephemeral, passing. This aspect of temporality is sometimes associated with notions of vanity, meaninglessness, absurdity and emptiness. But it also has a sense of the need to seize the moment, enjoy what is given, and use time well for work and pleasure.

Here is his classic statement on time:

> For everything there is a season, and a time for every matter under
>   heaven:
> a time to be born, and a time to die;
> a time to plant, and a time to pluck up what is planted;
> a time to kill, and a time to heal;

a time to break down, and a time to build up;
a time to weep, and a time to laugh;
a time to mourn, and a time to dance;
a time to throw away stones, and a time to gather stones together;
a time to embrace, and a time to refrain from embracing;
a time to seek, and a time to lose;
a time to keep, and a time to throw away;
a time to tear, and a time to sew;
a time to keep silence, and a time to speak;
a time to love, and a time to hate;
a time for war, and a time for peace. (Ecclesiastes 3.1-8)

He then gives a remarkable theological understanding of this. God has made 'everything suitable for its time'; yet the details of God's involvement in history are a mystery; and the practical lessons are to be happy and enjoy as long as we live, and to 'stand in awe' before God. Variations on these themes are played later in the book, with the vanity of life twinned repeatedly with affirmation, even in old age:

Light is sweet, and it is pleasant for the eyes to see the sun. Even those who live many years should rejoice in them all; yet let them remember that the days of darkness will be many. All that comes is vanity. (Ecclesiastes 11.7-8)

How is this wisdom of ordinary life to be connected with Luke's Gospel and Acts? Jesus' dramatic opening of his public ministry in the synagogue focuses on himself (in line with Isaiah 61) bringing good news to the poor, release to captives, sight to the blind, and freedom to the oppressed. Then he says: 'Today this scripture has been fulfilled in your hearing' (Luke 4.21). The basic teaching on time in Luke's writings is summed up there: the 'today' of Jesus is understood in continuity with the Old Testament, is filled with the realization of God's purposes through Jesus, and has at its heart good news for the poor and suffering. Past, present and future are reconfigured around the crucified and risen Jesus and his message of the kingdom of God.

This gives a pattern to time – it is striking that Luke portrays more of the key events celebrated in the Church Year than any other author – but above all it gives this person as the shaper of time. He teaches a wisdom about time. The basic matter is to recognize 'today' as a time inaugurating the kingdom of God and therefore setting priorities for everyone's desires, time and energy. Part of that is teaching about judgement, repentance and forgiveness, gratitude and the Sabbath.

Luke's distinctive understanding of time is even more subtle. In Acts, as well as perhaps in the Gospel, Luke looks back to the 'today' of the proclamation of Jesus as already 'past' for the reader in his own day. He is the first New Testament writer to conceive of the life and work of Jesus as already part of 'Christian history'. Indeed, his careful triple dating of the beginning of the ministry of Jesus in Luke 3.1-2 places the event in the public world of the rulers of Rome (Tiberius Caesar), Jewish political history (Herod, Philip and Lysanias the tetrarchs), and Jewish religious history (Annas and Caiaphas the high priests in *de jure* and *de facto* office). 'Today' becomes both a 'today' of the past that cannot be replicated in astronomical terms as in chronological time and a 'today' of destiny in this present in God's time and in human time.

Yet the future also colours Luke's understanding of 'today'. The world order of the political and social world is more important for Luke than in any other Gospel; nevertheless it stands under an expectation of a decisive event of grace and judgement in this final 'coming' (the *parousia*) of Jesus Christ at the end-time. This relativizes the permanence and finality of this world order, while at the same time affirming, rather than denying, the nature of embodied human life in the visible outer, public world. Luke does not diminish everything to some 'inner', private world of the heart. (This is the context for Luke's view of the vulnerable (the poor, women, outsiders), of time, of power and of the human attitude to poverty and riches.)

Yet more fundamental than the teaching is who Jesus is and what he does and undergoes. The events of his life, death, and resurrection show the reality of the 'Lord of the Sabbath' who is the Lord of time. These bear on the whole of history and the whole of the future. 'Perplexed', 'terrified', 'amazed', 'slow of heart to believe', 'hearts burning within us', 'startled and terrified', 'in their joy disbelieving and still wondering', 'great joy': those are some of the reactions of Jesus' followers in the last chapter of Luke as they begin to realize that this is the truth of 'today'. It was the beginning of a massive reorientation of their sense of time, life and death.

Ecclesiastes says that there is nothing better for mortals than receiving food and drink from the hand of God (Ecclesiastes 2.24, see above). Luke in the midst of these disturbing and epoch-making events shows Jesus giving signs of recognition and reassurance:

> When he was at the table with them, he took bread, blessed and broke it, and gave it to them. (Luke 24.30)

> … he showed them his hands and feet … They gave him a piece of broiled fish, and he took it and ate it in their presence. (Luke 24.40, 42)

... lifting up his hands, he blessed them. (Luke 24.50)

The response to that last blessing is the activity through which, above all, time can be well formed, hearts and minds fed, and wisdom related to her source:

... and they were continually in the temple blessing God.
(Luke 24.53)

Being human in new times

We have spoken above of the importance of pursing wisdom and of establishing good habits of mind, heart, imagination and will. In the course of this pursuit, Scripture has constantly been interpreted and reinterpreted through Christian history. Each new time has been characterized by conventions and constraints, ours no less than any earlier generation. Christian writers on these subjects have also recognized that understanding human nature and guiding it in the pursuit of the good have exercised the best minds of many civilizations, and that they had much to learn from sources external to the Jewish and Christian traditions. But this did not mean abandoning a Christian standpoint; indeed it was consistent with the example of the wisdom literature of the Old Testament, which was open to other traditions, notably from Egyptian sources. The biblical metaphor of 'plundering the Egyptians' (referring to the presents heaped on the Israelites to hasten their departure, Exodus 12.33-36) was widely used to interpret the borrowing from Greek philosophy which quickly became a feature of early Christian thought.

A notable example of this kind of activity was written in the last decade of the fourth century by a Greek bishop, named Nemesius, from Emesa, a town in Syria. It was a treatise, possibly not fully completed or revised, entitled *On the Nature of Human Being*, designed to commend a Christian view of humanity to reasonably learned, but not Christian people. Nemesius, of whose life we otherwise know nothing, shows himself to be well educated in classical philosophy and Greek medicine. As was so often the case, his work was later attributed to someone more famous – in fact to the prolific and celebrated Greek theologian, Gregory of Nyssa (*c*.330–*c*.395), whose name helped the treatise to survive. It was translated into Latin in the twelfth century and had a substantial influence on the Christian philosophy of the medieval period.

Two features of this work are especially notable. The first is the way in which Nemesius draws upon the views of classical philosophers, including Plato, Aristotle, the Stoics and Neoplatonists, in order to discuss what he regards as basic questions, such as the precise way in which soul and body are related in a human being. He accepts the validity of general arguments in philosophy, for example, for the creation of the universe by one God. But at the same time he uses these arguments to confirm what he regards as independently authoritative truths from Scripture. He places humanity on the boundary between two worlds, the physical (or phenomenal) and the spiritual (or intelligible). He treats it as an ordinary matter of observation that human beings are constantly dragged downwards by the desires of the flesh, and refers to the Genesis account of the Fall as consistent with this. Throughout the treatise there is an implicit understanding that in Christ the two worlds have been finally redeemed and reintegrated by the act of incarnation.

Thus, though there is a strong input from the philosophical psychology of the classical authors, the synthesis is undoubtedly governed by the Christian conclusions at which Nemesius arrives, sometimes despite his sources.

A second major feature which immediately strikes the modern reader is the extent of the biological and anatomical knowledge which the bishop displays. Medical biology was, of course, rooted in classical philosophy, and so was widely available to well-read people in addition to practitioners of medicine. But the reason which Nemesius gives for his interest is rather remarkable. It derives from his conviction that the union of soul and body is exceptionally close; so close, indeed, that before we can speak properly of the soul we must be well informed about the body. So in Nemesius' treatise on human being we read not merely about the faculties of imagination, intellect and will, or the passion of desire, grief, fear and anger, but also about digestion and nutrition, pulse and respiration, and the genitals and semen. What he offers, in short, is a fully articulated biological account of a human being within a philosophical and theological framework. In his comment on this William Telfer justifiably puts it in the following way: 'The seeker after a true ethic must ... go to school with the physicians and learn the facts of the body.' The wisdom which is being sought, one may say, is truly embodied. Indeed the whole point and purpose of the treatise is to be both clear and specific about the training which we need in order to establish in ourselves the habit of choosing the good and rejecting what is evil or inferior.

Nemesius' work was but one, albeit an influential, interpretation of the biblical account of the human situation, with the help of external philosophical sources. The point of going to so much trouble was to defend against alternative views the biblical assumption that human living confronts us with the reality and necessity of choice. It is required of us that we take deliberate action; our lives are not wholly predetermined by the stars or any other agency. Though the scope for free will is limited, it is nonetheless real. Because Nemesius desperately wanted to be persuasive to his readers on this subject, he takes them through the outline of a philosophical psychology from sources they would have acknowledged. This was how he attempted to demonstrate the consistency of the Christian way of wisdom with the best available thought.

This was one way of approaching the topic, but there was another, which took a stronger narrative cast, shaped in particular by the tradition from Augustine in the fifth century. Human being, it was taught, should be understood as having passed through certain states, each of which have left their mark. Fundamentally created in God's image and likeness, according to Genesis 1.26, humankind is nonetheless implicated in the consequences of the Fall. As a result, the guilt and penalty of original sin is passed from person to person, and is exacerbated by the law of God, and the inevitability of judgement. Nonetheless human nature has been embraced by the incarnate Son of God, by the merits and power of whose death and resurrection redemption is made possible. Transformation, therefore, is the newly realizable state of human being, experienced in part in this life through the grace of the Holy Spirit, but fulfilled in ultimate enjoyment of fellowship with God, the communion of saints in the eternal kingdom of heaven. The account is told as a sequence of events, but both the past (creation and Fall) and the future (redemption and fellowship with God) bear upon human being here and now. Though this narrative is not strictly incompatible with the more philosophical and psychological account we have encountered in Nemesius, the emphasis is much more strongly on the internal resources of Christian teaching to illuminate the task or journey of being human, through stages or states of being.

In both accounts, however, one can perceive a series of common themes, and because these play a role in our own approach to the topic we will make them explicit at this point.

1. The first is the orientation of the human being towards God, the capacity of a person for relationship with God. In the philosophical and psychological account, this is represented by the teaching on the soul. In narrative accounts, there is generally a speculative development of the implication of being made 'in the image and likeness of God'. Though it is misleading to characterize the first as Greek and the second as Hebrew, it is true that there is a substantial pre-Christian literature on the soul, which (as we have seen) plays an important role in how the soul is understood. The important and

common theme, however, is that human beings are inherently related to God, and are not merely material and mortal creatures.

2. As we have seen, the freedom of the will is a vital element in the philosophical literature, and its defence has remained central to Christian teaching through the ages. After Nemesius, in the teaching of Augustine and subsequently, the scope and character of this freedom has become controversial, for a reason which lies in the third common theme.

3. The third element is the fact that human being is drawn away from God by inordinate desire. In the narrative accounts, this is represented in the story of the Fall and its consequence, the presence of sin and death in the world. Christians have differed in the radicality with which they have interpreted the impact of sin upon human being. Augustine and those who have followed him strongly emphasize the mysterious solidarity in which being is engulfed, and attribute the movement back to God to the action of divine grace, before speaking of human freedom. The Greek tradition, by contrast, does not consider that human will is wholly overcome by evil and sin. Both traditions are obliged to consider the inescapability of death, and the threat of final separation from God.

4. For both accounts, however, repentance and the forgiveness of sins are both a real possibility and an actuality. Grace, conversion and transformation of life by the power of the Holy Spirit are thus a fundamental common theme in the two approaches.

5. Similarly, both accounts feature (in somewhat different ways) the attractiveness of the good, the joy of the risen life of fellowship with God through praise and worship, and the flowering of human potential in the communion of saints and a finally transfigured world. That human beings were created for this goal, links this theme with both creation and redemption.

These five themes play a vital role in our own work too, and link it to the tradition of how human beings have been understood through the Christian centuries. The fact that we have chosen to write on power, money, sex and time does not mean that we have forgotten the traditional themes of the soul, or the Fall, or the redemption through Christ, and we shall return to them in our final chapter. Our intention is rather both to listen to Scripture and to seek the way of wisdom in the context of a new time – a time in which understandings of power, money, sex and time shape human desires and perceptions in a way which sometimes seems to preclude the possibility of choice. We are exploring new ways into old territory.

Chapter 3
Power

Why are we writing about power in a report on human nature? The fundamental reason is that to be human is to have and to exercise powers of various kinds. It is also the case that there is a vast amount of teaching in the Bible about how to use these powers in an appropriate way. The Church, moreover, has a great deal of experience about the abuse of power, both as the abuser and the abused. Finally we need to write upon this subject precisely because it is complicated and full of puzzles and ambiguities; and because it is difficult to deal properly with either money or sex without clear ideas about power. (Time is less obviously connected; though, as we shall see, the powerful tend to have what is called 'valuable time' – literally so in the case of lawyers and others with scarce professional expertise.)

We have an obvious tendency to think of power as something big, abstract and distant. On one occasion, at a presentation of the topic, 'Money, sex and power', a member of the audience wryly and sadly remarked that she didn't think these subjects had very much to do with her. She was an older person, and explained that she was a widow living on a pension. Her response was certainly understandable. But it also illustrates the way in which all these matters only seem real to us in terms of their extremes; so to 'have money or power' means to be more than ordinarily wealthy or powerful.

This fact partially explains a very curious phenomenon in modern western democracies. It is plainly the case that never before in the history of western societies have ordinary citizens been given so much say in political life. At the same time, paradoxically, exactly the same people have come to see themselves as comparatively 'powerless', massively abstaining from the simplest forms of participation in public elections. As examples of who 'has power' they would doubtless name politicians, captains of industry, or opinion-formers in the media. To 'have power' means something exceptional. In this way 'power' has become almost an object or a thing, far removed from the abilities or capacities possessed by every living being, and at least to some degree by every citizen in a democracy.

What do we mean by 'power'? How is it to be defined? There are two rather different approaches to this question in the vast literature on this topic. One way is to attempt to be as precise as possible and to differentiate between it and other similar words, such as 'influence' and 'authority'. Another way is to accept the imprecision of ordinary speech, and to invite the reader to attend to the particular meanings of the word in particular contexts. In this chapter we have decided to follow the latter course. To get the discussion under way we can adopt a limited or minimal understanding of the term 'power' to mean the production of effects. Moreover the specific context in which we propose to set our understanding of power is that of Christian theology. The interest we have in this subject – and it is widely acknowledged that the concept of power is related to and reflects particular interests – is the puzzle of what 'having power' has become in the modern world.

One of the beneficial consequences of considering the issue of power in a theological context is that it restores the ordinariness of the subject. It is because everyone without exception is thought of in relation to God, a God of power and might, that involvement in God's power is inescapable. There are, of course, complexities and objections to consider to this formulation, which this chapter will examine in due course. But the claim is at least intelligible. If Christians are 'participants in the divine nature' (2 Peter 1.4), and if power belongs to the divine nature, then Christians, and potentially all humanity, may share that power. The feeling, understandable though it may have been in context, that 'power' has nothing to do with an 'ordinary person' is based on a mistake. On the contrary, it would not be possible to give an account of human beings in God's sight without offering some positive and serious reflection on the powers bestowed on all of God's creatures, on the power of God in the achievement of human redemption, and on participation through faith, hope and love in God's own being.

Power, a male concept?

A fundamental objection to our subject as a whole must be considered, which is that the very concept of power is intrinsically distorted by having been developed in a patriarchal context in the interests of men. By 'patriarchy' in this context we understand the practice and the assumption that a man or men of seniority are to rule within households or whole societies. On this understanding the fact that God is spoken of in Judaism and Christianity as a 'God of power and might' is simply further evidence that dominant males have imposed a male view of God. Men, it is said, tend to think of themselves as isolated and in competition with others. God, for Jews and Christians, is a jealous God who will brook no rivals. He – for that is the personal pronoun which the tradition predominantly uses – is complete in himself and dwells in unapproachable light (1 Timothy 6.1-6). God is spoken of as King, judge, Lord, father, each of which are terms redolent of male power. Human beings, by contrast, are small, low and of no account, and can only approach this God with awe and humility. Concepts of power derived from this tradition are distorted from the first; the only way to free oneself from them is to replace them with alternatives.

Two aspects of this critique are persuasive. In the first place the evidence that women and men tend to conceive their identities in differing ways is strong. The interpretation of this divergence is disputed. Some place great emphasis on the evolved biological roles of males and females; others point to the way in which societies construct these roles and train men and women to adopt them. Whichever is the case, and it may be that elements of both are true, it hardly seems plausible to rank the male viewpoint above the female, or vice versa. If the way men and women conceive their identities is genuinely different, then those differences require equal emphasis and valuation.

Secondly, there is important evidence, to which we turn shortly, of a serious, culturally imposed distortion of the notion of power, equating it with domination. An instance of this is illuminating. In a mid-twentieth-century work on power translated into English, a sentence reads, 'A man feels himself more of a man when he is imposing himself and making others the instruments of his will' (Bertrand de Jouvenal, *Power*, 1952). The sentence perfectly encapsulates the dominative tendency in modern ways of thinking about power. But because the English translator unhappily chose the term 'man' to render an original which was unmistakably applied to both sexes, the extract was chosen to illustrate the problem of male dominance in the programme notes of a recent performance of Shakespeare's *The Taming of the Shrew*. (One of us also recalls a library copy of the same text in which a commentary appeared in pencil in the margin, 'True of men, but hardly of women.')

It is, however, a very partial reading of the biblical tradition to describe God as relishing a male separateness. It is true that God's creatures are instructed to purify their hearts before approaching God; but it is also taught, 'Draw near to God, and he will draw near to you' (James 4.8). After the forgiveness of sins there exists genuine fellowship (*koinonia*) with God (1 John 1.6-7). Abraham, indeed, is said to have been a friend of God (James 2.23), and the love of God bestows the status of friends upon Jesus' disciples (John 15.12-17). There is undeniably an important point in alertness to male bias in religious traditions written and largely (though not exclusively) interpreted by men, but strands of the tradition do not match so generalized a criticism.

Power as domination

Consistent with the tendency to evaluate – and to demonize – money, sex and power by reference to extreme examples of each is the habit of identifying power with domination. That domination, the imposition of the will of one agent and another, is a form of power, is undeniable. But are the two concepts interchangeable? The problem is that in ordinary usage the word has a range of meanings. Quite a few of these have negative connotations, 'power-games', 'power-politics', 'power struggles', for example. Others, as we have already observed, are perfectly neutral. A person who can speak has 'the power of speech'. The multiple abilities or capacities of human beings, natural or acquired, can be spoken of, quite appropriately, as powers. Speech, however, offers a good example of the tendency to see power in threatening or negative terms. Someone who can not merely speak, but can speak persuasively in public, may be understood as having power in a rather abstract kind of way, inspiring in some admiration, and in others suspicion. It would be oddly at variance with ordinary usage if at a certain stage in a spectrum of rhetorical ability one speaker was said to exercise 'power', while another was merely talking. Both surely are deploying the power of speech, but in certain cases the intentions and the scale of the consequences may require rigorous scrutiny.

It is consistent with this broad use of the word that we can identify positive uses of the term. This is notably the case in the complex term 'empowerment', generally regarded in a positive light. A person or group of persons are empowered when their situation is changed from a lack of certain freedoms to a capacity to exercise autonomous choice. It is characteristically and appropriately used of marginal or oppressed groups in society. The assumption is that positive countervailing power can be mobilized against dominative power; in which case the concept of power cannot be intrinsically negative or simply identified with domination. There are solid advantages in preserving the plural 'powers', and supplementing the potentially abstract singular 'power'. It is perfectly normal and appropriate in many contexts for people to exercise powers of various kinds and degrees of effectiveness. In some cases, but not necessarily all, scrutiny and suspicion are appropriate; there are instances where the use of certain powers has become dominative. But it is a misuse of the word to equate it with domination.

Power as authority

One of the consequences of equating power and domination is that it becomes necessary for there to be a word without negative overtones to speak of the kind of influence which is morally legitimate. For many people that word is 'authority'. But is authority a kind of power, or something to be contrasted with power? Much depends upon definition, and in this context examples are very useful.

What is the authority of the police? Law bestows on them the right to arrest people under certain tightly specified conditions. This entitlement also includes the right to use violent means if absolutely necessary. But a good deal of their authority is more nebulous than that. It can be used to settle disputes, for example, or to prevent matters from escalating into crimes. That kind of authority can be abused as well. In ordinary speech about this complex situation it seems perfectly natural to speak of the powers of the police, but to use the word 'authority' of those powers which have a clear legal or more broadly moral basis. This enables one to say that if the police engage in disreputable activities, they retain their powers but lose important elements of their (moral) authority. 'Power' and 'authority' are not therefore to be used simply as though they were alternative terms, one negative and one positive. A reasonable way of understanding the term 'authority' is to see it as a case in which the power which is exercised is backed by some kind of claimed justification or legitimacy.

This common-sense way of seeing the relationship between the two words is strongly confirmed by their use in English New Testament translations. Of the three Greek words commonly translated by 'power' one, *exousia*, is regularly rendered as 'authority'. Thus, in Mark and Luke, Jesus is said to teach 'with authority' – the implication being that despite lack of formal authorization, there was real justification for his words in the commission and inspiration of the Holy Spirit. In Luke (4.36), however, speaking of Jesus' exorcisms the two words are used together ('with authority and power – *dynamis* – he commands the unclean spirits'). The word *dynamis* has already been used by Luke, and is so frequently, in the phrase 'the power of the Spirit' (4.14). The distinction is one of nuance, not of contrast, still less of alternatives. How power came to be equated with domination needs to be explained.

Power in western Christian thought

The contribution made by Christian thinkers to the understanding of power came about as a result of the extraordinary change of circumstances for the fourth-century Church following the conversion to Christianity of the emperor, Constantine, in AD 313. Though in many parts of the empire Christians had begun both to be tolerated and to play significant roles in public life, persecution was always a possibility and, under Emperor Diocletian in 303, a reality. It is claimed by Henry Chadwick that the 'accession of a Christian emperor marks no great divide in the development of Christian thinking about government, power, coercion, and war'. That may be so. But it must be remembered that new circumstances always provoked rereadings of the Scriptures, both Old and New Testaments, and that the scriptural treasury was generously stocked.

In particular, the young New Testament Christian communities' sense of themselves as the 'people of God', living in obedience to a new covenant, and acknowledging a unique sovereign, was deeply influenced by the narratives and experiences of the Old Testament. These include, of course, remarkably different episodes; the migration of Abraham, slavery in and liberation from Egypt, a wilderness experience, the infiltration, conquest and settlement of the Holy Land, the regimes of more or less unsatisfactory judges and kings, the establishment of the Davidic dynasty, episodes of assimilation to and revulsion from local culture, invasion, subjugation and exile, restoration and rebuilding. In their distinctive interpretation of the Old Testament, the early Christian communities inherited a vast resource of texts dealing with power in virtually all its forms; the power of God in creation and history, God's vulnerability to challenge, God's support of warfare, the power of anointed kings and priests, criticism of the abuse of wealth and the perversion of justice, concern for the oppressed, enslaved and marginalized, ambiguous relations with powerful nations and imperial tyrants, movements of withdrawal into poverty and ritual holiness, longings for a powerful deliverer and for God's final establishment of true justice on earth. All these are reflected in the texts and were available for Christian retrieval. Sometimes the interpretation was transformed by reflection upon the New Testament witness; at other times it was simply transplanted.

The Book of Psalms, which because of its use in worship had already acquired multiple resonances in widely differing circumstances, had long been a fruitful source of Christian interpretation. The crucifixion itself was understood through two psalms (22 and 31), among others, detailing both intense suffering and rescue. The former indeed finishes with a song of triumph:

> All the ends of the earth shall remember
> and turn to the Lord;
> And all the families of the nations
> shall worship before him.
> For dominion belongs to the Lord,
> and he rules over the nations. (Psalm 22.27-28)

The celebration of the power of God in creation, redemption and final restoration is constantly being reinforced by the liturgical use of the Psalms.

The Church did not have to wait long for an interpretation of the significance of its newly converted emperor. On the thirtieth anniversary of Constantine's reign (335/6), Eusebius, bishop of Caesarea and prominent Church historian, delivered a remarkable speech of praise. In it Constantine's accession is not merely celebrated as providential; he enjoys, so Eusebius asserts, a special relationship with God through the divine Word, the *Logos*. The speech was a performance likely to appeal not merely to a Christian audience in that it drew upon late Greek philosophical resources. In these texts earthly monarchs were said to embody replicas of the kingship of Zeus, and themselves to be gods among men. Although such thoughts were impossible for Christians, nonetheless, as St Paul had taught, 'those authorities that exist have been instituted by God' (Romans 13.1). If in Greek thought the king had been guided by the reason or *Logos* of true philosophy, why should not a Christian king be animated by the *Logos* of God? Significantly, in making this claim for this occasion, Eusebius failed to speak personally of Christ.

This interpretive structure, with its positive evaluation of power in the hands of a Christian emperor, exerted a massive influence in Byzantine political theory for a thousand years. In one sense it was not new, in that earlier Christian thinkers had seen the simultaneous appearance of Jesus Christ and Caesar Augustus as an act of divine providence assisting the spread of the Christian gospel. But through the accession of a Christian emperor the opportunities for the deliberate exercise of power and patronage had been hugely increased, as the bishops of the Church were quickly to discover. It is notable that three-quarters of a century later, after substantial experience of imperial power, Augustine of Hippo (354–430) in the West was to offer a much cooler evaluation of the significance of Constantine's appearance and activities.

Though Eusebius deployed Old Testament prophecies of deliverance and rescue as well as New Testament Logos theology in his interpretation, there was one acute danger in his thought, the loss of an eschatological perspective (that is, of God's final verdict upon human history). The problem with the late Greek metaphysical scheme is that it involved an altogether too complete realization of divine activity in the person of the emperor. If the emperor was a kind of manifestation of God's sovereign rule over the world, how could one resist or criticize him when he did wrong? The advantage of Christian eschatology was that it recognized that the rule of Christ had not yet been established.

We still live in times of ignorance, negligence and outright wickedness. Even professedly Christian emperors are prone to temptations.

It was specifically Augustine's achievement to incorporate eschatology in a vital way in his political interpretation of power. But then circumstances had radically changed – indeed they were changing throughout the thirteen years in which his major work, *The City of God* (413–27), was being written. In the early years of the fifth century, the sense of the triumph of Christian faith ('the whole world has become a choir praising Christ', Augustine had rejoiced) rapidly receded under the impact of the barbarian successes in the western provinces of the empire. These culminated in the sack of Rome in 410. It became urgent for western Christians to consider how such reverses could be possible, given the providential role of the empire. Augustine's sophisticated and remarkable solution is the doctrine of the eschatological 'City of God', citizenship of which involves participation with the angels in the true worship of God. It is contrasted with 'the earthly city', and proposes two completely contrasted orientations of the desires of the human heart. Characteristic of the earthly city is the proud lust for power; typical of the heavenly city is a concern for the common good for the sake of a heavenly society.

What then of Christian rulers? Augustine's answer is that if (and it is a significant condition) they are skilled in the art of good government, then there is nothing better for humanity than that they should wield power. But they always fall short of perfect righteousness, and their reward is no greater than that of the humblest of the saints. In the mere fact of power itself there is nothing wrong. Fault arises simply in the souls of those who love their own power without regard to the true justice of the omnipotent God. Augustine stops short of telling his readers what the true love of justice would mean in practice for a Christian ruler, and this may well be an evasion of a serious difficulty.

Against the background of this contrast and conflict of the two cities, Augustine sets the whole of human existence in a consciously dramatized way. The struggle is much more subtle than that of simple myths like *Star Wars*. The fault line, so to speak, runs through each individual heart. So there are good Roman leaders, such as Caesar and Cato, who while striving for glory were able to follow the example of virtue to a degree. The problem was their love of praise, which spoiled their achievement.

Commentators often rightly use the word 'ambivalence' to describe Augustine's contribution to the understanding of power. But it was a complex and relatively unsystematized mode of thought which fatally had already made room for coercion in religious matters. In the light of subsequent history of religious persecution in the West it can be no afterthought to acknowledge that Augustine supported and justified the forcible conversion of the Donatists, a widespread Christian sect-like movement in North Africa and elsewhere. It was a policy for which no conceivable New Testament justification could be offered; the use of the text 'compel people to come in' (Luke 14.23), from Jesus' parable, offered the flimsiest of pretexts. For Augustine it was a matter of administering correction or discipline, so that stubborn wills might be broken. It was like the administration of nasty medicine for a patient's good. And it was essentially the Church's own discipline, acting through Christian officials. In Augustine's mind there was no thought of a principled separation between Church and State, or of separable duties and responsibilities. Modern commentators have developed the concept of 'political augustinianism' to designate the exceptionally influential thought that, at least in political theory, the Church ought to absorb the State.

Discipline, moreover, had one other form, and power another sphere of legitimate exercise, in the task of pastoral care. Himself deeply influenced by Augustine, Pope Gregory the Great formulated in his *Pastoral Rule* (*c.*591) a psychologically perceptive set of guidelines for preserving humility whilst engaged in the tasks of leadership in the Church. It exercised vast influence throughout the early Middle Ages and was used not merely by bishops and abbots, but also by Christian kings and other leaders. In England it was translated by Alfred the Great in the late tenth century and formed the model for the exercise of power in public life for centuries.

Implicit in this structure, however, was a difficulty. What if the perception of the interests of the Christian commonweal differed between secular or religious leaders? How would the respective domains of sacred and secular power negotiate their differences? Was there any limit to the scope of their respective jurisdictions? This was to become a principal issue when a sophisticated forger, Isidorus Mercator (known as Pseudo-Isidore), forged and falsified papal letters so as to demonstrate that the Church had been ruled from the earliest days by papal decrees.

On the face of it there were two distinct powers, that of bishops and that of kings. 'Christ', wrote Pope Gelasius to Emperor Anastasius I in 494, 'separated the offices of both powers according to their proper activities and their special dignities, so that Christian emperors would have need of bishops in order to attain eternal life and bishops would have recourse to imperial direction in the conduct of temporary affairs'

(*Tractate* IV, 11). Medieval writers from the ninth century onwards liked to illustrate this distinction by referring to the passage in the Gospel of Luke, where, in the Upper Room, the disciples told Jesus that they had two swords. Jesus replied, 'It is enough' (Luke 22.38), and this (ambiguous) response was taken to support the need for the two 'swords' of the spiritual and temporal powers. The difficulty was, however, that bishops – especially popes – considered it their prerogative to instruct kings in their duty, and to correct them if they did wrong. The spiritual power is thus the greater because, though it has temporal application, it is not merely temporal. Or so Pope Gregory VII (1073–85) and his reformers insisted. And it was none other than Bernard of Clairvaux (1090–1153), a noted abbot and spiritual writer, who in a letter to a pope who had once been a novice under his direction assured him that he was called to the 'fullness of power' (*plenitudo potestatis*). Both the swords, therefore, belong to the Church: the spiritual sword is unsheathed by the Church, the temporal for the Church.

This doctrine was strenuously resisted by emperors, kings and their apologists, and no less energetically supported by popes and their theologians from the twelfth to the fifteenth century. These now largely forgotten centuries saw countless treatises on spiritual and temporal power. Though occasionally the Latin term *auctoritas* (authority) was used for the former, for the most part the debate concerned *potestas* (power). Nor was it mere theory and hot air. The papacy claimed the right to depose emperors and kings, or to release their subjects from oaths of allegiance, for very serious crimes. This happened under Pope Innocent IV in 1245; in 1302 Pope Boniface VIII (1294–1303) produced a bull, *Unam Sanctam*, asserting the pope's right to an unshared headship as the vicar of Christ upon earth. Whatever he judges to be good is good; obedience to what he decides is essential to salvation; his jurisdiction covers every aspect of morality in temporal affairs.

This history has been recalled as a reminder that for centuries Christian theologians including the popes had no difficulty with the thought that the Church must be involved in the exercise of power, both in its own life in the form of pastoral rule and in its relationships with the temporal or secular world of government. Although when we read Augustine with care, we see in his work considerably more ambivalence about the matter than later centuries did, his influence both direct and as refracted through Gregory the Great is everywhere. How then has it come about that the term 'power' has now such negative connotations – as some modern research has now demonstrated? In a way the answer is obvious. We have become appalled by the history of religious coercion, notably despite all apologetics, by the Crusades, the Inquisition, the persecution of the Anabaptists, the burning of witches, and the justification long into the twentieth century of the theory that 'error has no rights'. Furthermore the twentieth century witnessed such miseries inflicted by gross dictators on their populations that we have earned the right to be suspicious of every form of power; as the historian, Lord Acton, famously said, 'All power tends to corrupt, and absolute power corrupts absolutely.'

The protest against power

The response to *Unam Sanctam* was not long in coming. First the lay Italian poet Dante in a treatise on Monarchy (1312), then Marsilius of Padua (1275–1348) produced a remarkable analysis and refutation of the papal claim to plenitude of power, based on a combination of arguments from both Aristotle and the New Testament. Marsilius not merely denied the divine origin of the papal office; he asserted the necessity of a single source of all jurisdiction, including the power of coercion, namely the whole body of the citizens. Needless to say the book was banned shortly after its production, but had a wide but secret influence on subsequent discussion. Henry VIII had the treatise translated into English, and a version, shorn of its references to popular sovereignty, circulated widely in England at the Reformation.

A very different type of response emerged some two hundred years later, from another Italian, Nicholo Machiavelli (1469–1527). Just on the brink of European reformation, he wrote an astonishing work of political psychology, called *The Prince* (1513, first published 1532), which absolutely parted company with the moral outlook of the Christian tradition. It scandalized and was denounced by Catholics and (in due course) Protestants alike; for Shakespeare, Machiavelli is the source of the ideas guiding an Iago in *Othello* or an Edmund in *King Lear*. 'Machiavellian' has come simply to mean devious or tricky. When people use the word 'political' in a negative sense, it is because of the connotation that the exercise of power in the public realm is bound to involve the disregard of ordinary personal ethics.

What Machiavelli wants of government – and he lived in the highly unstable world of the Borgia popes and the Medici princes – is, above all, stability and public contentment. It would be desirable, he says, if the Church could have set the standard of how to govern. But Pope Alexander VI (1492–1503) had, in his view, forfeited all right to be regarded as an example. There was no alternative to studying carefully the art of political survival. This, he claimed, had to be based on the working assumption that most human beings were fickle, greedy and self-interested, and that one's rivals were all potential assassins. It is not that Christian virtues do not apply in their own sphere; it is rather, that politics is an altogether different matter. Because human goodness is essentially unpredictable, a prince who wants to provide his people with the good of a stable government is bound to act on the general belief in human wickedness. It is that knowledge of human psychology which justifies, Machiavelli makes clear, occasional displays of exemplary and ruthless violence from the prince.

The interpretation and evaluation of Machiavelli's contribution to political thought is still massively controversial. But a consistent strand runs through much western political thought since Machiavelli, which is this negativity about human beings. It was, if anything, underscored by the main European reformers who reappropriated Augustine's doctrine of original sin. But in their cases there remained a positive evaluation of what a Christian prince or magistrate might be able to achieve. On the whole it was the thought of Marsilius rather than Machiavelli which guided Protestant responses. But from the sixteenth century onwards a new 'realism' had entered specifically political thought, and in this context the concept of 'power' subtly changed. Where the assumption had been for centuries that Christian leaders might properly exercise power because in doing so they were, or could be, participating in God's own purposes, the suspicion grew that power itself was always tainted because it involved the exercise of the dominative will of one person over another. Though not every example of political thinking exhibited this tendency, nonetheless it became increasingly common to equate power with domination; to the point that the mere utterance of the word 'power' became a signal for a negative response.

A further characteristic of modern thought contributed, though somewhat paradoxically, to the same negativity. This was the proposal or assumption that there was only a specific and finite amount of power in circulation, with the consequence that if one person had more of it, then another had correspondingly less. In this way the possession of power came to be seen as necessarily the outcome of a struggle to advance or protect one's own interests. The negativity arises from the assumption, for that is what it is, that the definition of one's interests is bound to involve overt or covert self-aggrandizement. But the paradox lies in the fact that, frequently enough, the analysis of an imbalance of power is carried out allegedly in the interests of those with less power; their acquisition of further power is regarded as a positive achievement.

Christian thought has been fully involved in these developments, at least in their early stages. Marsilius of Padua's challenge to the papal doctrine of plenitude of power contains striking reference to the biblical story of the dispute about which disciple was to be most prominent and Jesus' saying about service (Mark 10.35-45; Matthew 20.20-28; Luke 22.24-27). There is just a contradiction, he asserts, between the pope's claim that the spiritual sword is superior to the temporal, and Jesus' contrast between worldly domination ('rulers lord it over' their subjects) and the example of service set by himself to his disciples ('not so among you'). Luther, who may or may not have read Marsilius, says exactly the same thing, formulating, as so often, a memorable sound-bite, 'not power but service'.

But, of course, the issue for Christian princes and magistrates was not so clear, as Luther was to discover. During the Peasants' War of 1524-6, and sensing the threat to the whole of the young Reformation, he acts without inhibition on the assumption that as a spiritual leader he can call on the temporal sword to crush incipient revolution. At this stage there is no negativity attaching to power as such, except that it must not be directly exercised by Church leaders themselves. But that was enough to give power a certain 'secularity', which was of course, to increase with time. It is also true that more modern sensibility becomes concerned about the gusto with which Luther defends the possibility that a Christian might have a vocation to be the government's hangman.

This secularizing tendency was strongly reinforced by the evolution of the social sciences from the nineteenth century onwards. Originally proclaimed as a conscious, scientific alternative to a theological-speculative understanding of human social behaviour, they have at the very least understood themselves as value-free. A celebrated definition of power from the doyen of early twentieth-century sociologists, Max Weber (1864–1920), strongly confirms the realist trend initiated by Machiavelli. Weber wrote in acknowledgement of an indebtedness to another master of suspicion, Friedrich Nietzsche. For Nietzsche there was a gulf between what people say and what people do. They may say, 'service, service, service' or 'love, love, love', but underneath there is an unacknowledged 'will-to-power' in operation covering its self-interest in layers of rationalization. Freud's revelations about the workings of the unconscious tended in the same direction.

When Bertrand Russell, writing on power just before the Second World War, offered the gloomy view that 'of the infinite desires of man, the chief are the desires for power and glory', he was standing in a long tradition of western political thought and social science. Machiavelli, Thomas Hobbes and Nietzsche had said similar things, but, as we have seen, so had Augustine. The difference was that Augustine believed that set in the human heart was another impulse and another longing; that human beings had been made by God, indeed for fellowship with God; and that, though difficult, it was not impossible for a true Christian to exercise God-given power to God's glory. But to an ever-increasing degree Christian thinkers have ceased to offer an alternative account, credible in the light of Machiavelli and Nietzsche, though they have the resources to do so.

Omnipotence and the redefinition of power

It has already been said that one of the very striking consequences of adopting a theological view of power is that it restores the ordinariness of the subject. God is blessed in Anglican worship in words put into the mouth of King David at the dedication of gifts for the Temple of Jerusalem:

> Yours, O Lord, are the greatness, the power, the glory, the victory, and the majesty; for all that is in the heavens and on the earth is yours. (1 Chronicles 29.11)

Similar words are used in some of the most familiar versions of the Lord's Prayer:

> For the kingdom and the power and the glory are yours, for ever, Amen. (Matthew 6.13)

The linking of heaven and earth is highly significant. As Job pointed out, even the most stunning aspects of the visible creation reveal 'but the outskirts of his ways' (Job 26.14). What is praised is a kingdom and a rule beyond what is evident here and now, though it *is* to be seen and experienced here and now. The act of praising anticipates, as it were, an order of things which is yet to be revealed, but of whose reality we are fully convinced. The power of God in his kingdom or rule impinges on our lives in its smallest details and at every turn; it is in that sense ordinary. But there is a greater glory to be revealed, one which sheds its extraordinary light on even the most mundane parts of our lives.

The expression, 'Almighty God', is very commonplace in the Church's prayers, as we know. Though the expression is commoner in the Old Testament, where it can also be translated 'Lord of hosts', than in the New Testament, it has become exceptionally familiar in Christian prayers, creeds and hymns. The Latin translation of the Greek word for almighty (*panto-krator*) is *omni-potens*; and it was not long before the philosophical tradition of the West was asserting that omnipotence was one of the attributes of God. But in what sense can omnipotence be ascribed to God? Is it not undermined or contradicted by the plain evidence of evil and suffering in God's world? How, moreover, can it be reconciled with what appears, at least, to be the reality of human freedom? And surely the idea of omnipotence must be reassessed in thought of the passion and crucifixion of Jesus, if Jesus is indeed the one whom the Church confesses him to be, 'God from God, light from light, true God from true God, one in being with the Father'. These difficulties, it must be said, are very well known in the history of theology and have constantly been considered. They have been strongly reinforced in the modern period by concern for the integrity, not just of freedom of the will, but of nature itself as understood by contemporary science.

The Doctrine Commission has already written on this matter in its report, *We Believe in God* (pp. 148–56). One reviewer concluded on reading these pages, 'God is not as powerful as he used to be.' It would have been more accurate to say that the God who is praised in the Bible and in the prayers of the Church as possessing greatness, power and glory does enable human beings to be free, does encounter hostility and contradiction, and does not bring all opposition to an end by a blinding flash of sheer power. To that extent, some ideas implicit in the term 'omnipotence' are misleading. It has always been realized that it was scandalous and difficult to say that the Son of the omnipotent God was scourged and hung on a cross until he died.

At the very least we must say that the teaching of the Bible about the power of God is internally complex. It is important to remember that the praise of God's power is an anticipation of a state of affairs to come. This power cannot simply be excised from theology as an embarrassment, or trimmed back in order to make more room for human powers or the powers of nature. The confident attribution of power to God stands for two vital truths in Christian teaching, both with practical implications; first, that nothing in this life ever escapes God's sovereignty, just as nothing in creation is self-originating or self-sufficient. God is the alpha and omega of all that is; in Paul's understanding of the final outcome of human history, every ruler, authority and power is to be ended by Christ in his kingdom, and then, finally, the Son with himself be subject to the Father, 'so that God may be all in all' (1 Corinthians 15.24-28). This is the final ground of confidence in God whatever happens, and of the praised God in all circumstances.

Second, the attribution of power to God is deliberately intended to cut the pretensions of human beings (especially of tyrants) down to size. Jesus' reply to Pilate, 'You would have no power over me unless it had been given you from above' (John 19.11), is a classic instance of this truth, which has sustained many in the throes of persecution.

It is not, therefore, too much to say that, as we have already suggested, the incarnation, passion, death and resurrection of Christ redefine the biblical understanding of power in far-reaching and subtle ways. Though the passion and crucifixion reveal the vulnerability and weakness of Christ, that is not all there is to be said. The self-giving of the Son of God to death is itself presented in Scripture as a triumph and an act of strength. Similarly, the Resurrection is not presented merely as a cancelling out of the death, by an act of triumphant power. It is the public vindication of the death itself. Paul explains that it was because of his grace that Christ became poor (2 Corinthians 8.9), so that the weakness of the crucifixion is not the reversal of an unfortunate accident from a position of strength, but is a mark precisely of that grace. Exactly this point was clear to a fourth-century theologian, Gregory of Nyssa, who wrote of the Incarnation:

> The fact that the omnipotent nature should have been capable of descending to the low estate of humanity provides a clearer proof of power than great and supernatural miracles. (*Catechetical Orations* 24)

A similar thought passed into a ninth-century Collect, and from there into the Anglican tradition of public prayer:

> Almighty God, who declarest thy almighty power most chiefly in showing mercy and pity ... (Collect for the 11th Sunday after Trinity, *Book of Common Prayer* and *Common Worship*)

In the light of such evidence it cannot simply be asserted that traditional theology was unaware of the need for essential qualifications in explicating the doctrine of divine omnipotence.

Ancient writers were also alert to the implications of confessing the love of God, and struggled to present God's 'impassibility' in relation to it. But the way of love, as described for example in 1 Corinthians 13, also bears vitally upon the issue of power. The sort of love which is patient and kind, and which hopes and endures all things, is absolutely different in quality and tone from an aggressive exercise of dominating power. The example of the 'meekness and gentleness' of Christ was never far from the mind of Paul (2 Corinthians 10.1), even though he held that he had ample cause for coming to his difficult and quarrelsome congregation with a stick in his hand (1 Corinthians 4.21). What we are witnessing in these passages is the practical outcome of redefining God's power in the light of the Incarnation.

It is again extraordinary that the Gospels tell the story of Jesus' anguish in the Garden of Gethsemane, as the implications of his betrayal and desertion become clear to him. Jesus' consciously reached decision after his inner struggle is to make himself vulnerable to arrest, to a farcical series of trials, and finally to crucifixion. When Peter took up a weapon in defence, Jesus refused the option of force, including the supreme assistance of 'twelve legions of angels' (Matthew 26.53). This chosen vulnerability is a challenge of immense range and significance to the instinct of all who exercise powers, even quite modest ones, to barricade themselves behind walls of invulnerability to disturbance and criticism. But to follow Christ in the pathway of his passion is to accept and to practise the pattern of his vulnerability.

Conflict and empowerment

Human life is set within the context of the kingdom of heaven, and human beings are necessarily involved in its conflicts. The fight, according to the Letter to the Ephesians,

> is not against enemies of blood and flesh, but against the rulers, against the authorities, against the cosmic powers of this present darkness, against the spiritual forces of evil in the heavenly places. (Ephesians 6.12)

The classical Christian tradition took up this passage in numerous writings about spiritual warfare, and it has appealed to many in the monastic tradition, in Puritanism and in the contemporary charismatic movement. It is not without its problems and difficulties, as the history of exorcism abundantly demonstrates. The claiming of 'signs and wonders' as an integral part of 'power evangelism' has already been discussed in the Report of the Doctrine Commission, *We Believe in the Holy Spirit* (1991, pp. 103-7) and does not need to be extensively rehearsed. There is a proper balance to be struck; 'Christians', that report argued, 'must expect the way of the cross as well as the power of the resurrection ... Thus triumphalism is illegitimate, for we have not yet arrived. Equally defeatism is inappropriate, for we are not where we were' (p. 107).

It follows from this that Christians, who have as their resource the gift of 'power from on high' (Luke 24.49), should never see themselves as literally powerless. Though their weapons are 'not from this world' (John 18.36), they are equipped and empowered for their fight. The celebration of 'powerlessness', which can occasionally be encountered in contemporary theology, though well meant, is in fact misleading. Its intention is to be a form of identification with the 'weakness' of the crucified Christ, and with those on the margins of society, the comparatively powerless. But the difficulty is that it apparently accepts an inadequate understanding of power, rather than engages in the redefinition of power required by the Incarnation. It can also be of very little comfort to those who have little power. The liberation of the marginalized entails the exercise of some kind of power; it is precisely the re-evaluation of power which may enable the comparatively powerless to exercise power in their own terms. Though identification with the marginal has a vital point, the transformation of their situation is the goal, and that goal involves 'empowerment' of some kind. Quietism, pessimism or despair is no solution.

The abuse of power

Nonetheless it is an integral part of the biblical portrayal of power that its abuse is an ever-present temptation and possibility. A more extraordinary feature of the Old Testament than is sometimes realized, and quite unlike that quantity of ancient literature whose function is to legitimate the power of the established elites, is the realistic warning attached to the institution of kingship (1 Samuel 8). Saul, though chosen by God and anointed by Samuel, was rejected for his disobedience; David, his successor, was unmasked by the prophet Nathan, for an act of gross abuse of power (2 Samuel 12). Then the prophets clearly identify injustice to the poor as disobedience to the law of God (Amos 2-5; Isaiah 1).

Use of the sacred literature, therefore, is a constant reminder of the danger of power. Correspondingly there is commendation attached to the virtue of humility. 'The fear of the Lord', says the Book of Proverbs, is a training in wisdom, and the way to honour is humility (Proverbs 15.33). 'It is better to be of a lowly spirit among the poor than to divide the spoil with the proud' (Proverbs 16.19).

This teaching strengthens itself in a pattern of reversal, in which characterizes God's own activity. The most familiar example is contained in the Magnificat:

> He has shown strength with his arm
> and has scattered the proud in their conceit,
> casting down the mighty from their thrones
> and lifting up the lowly.
> He has filled the hungry with good things
> and sent the rich away empty. (*Common Worship*; Luke 1.51-53)

Exactly the same pattern is to be found in Hannah's prayer in the Old Testament (1 Samuel 2.7-8):

> The Lord makes poor and makes rich;
> he brings low, he also exalts.
> He raises up the poor from the dust;
> he lifts the needy from the ash heap,
> to make them sit with princes
> and inherit a seat of honour.
> For the pillars of the earth are the Lord's,
> and on them he has set the world.

It is evident that what lies behind these examples is a relationship to God's power, not simply a way of responding to one's own or another's powers. To have confidence in God's power, exercised as providence and trustworthiness in creation, is to be freed from the anxiety which fuels self-assertion. Human beings suffer chronically from anxiety, and anxiety lies behind the desire to dominate over others and thus limit their capacity to exercise power over us. This is why Jesus' repeated invitation to his followers not to be anxious lies at a very fundamental level in the understanding and exercise of God-given powers in human relationships.

The Church and worldly power

Power is recognizably distributed and exercised in the Church, as much in the Early Church as today. Within the Church some people have greater access than others to decision-making power, and this is as true of so-called 'non hierarchical' Churches, as of openly hierarchical ones. An unfortunate result of adopting the slogan, 'Not power but service', is to disguise the way in which powers are exercised, sometimes disastrously even from those who plainly possess them. In this matter gossip and jokes about Church life are a much more reliable guide to the real state of affairs, than a misleading theology. A very large Church is bound, for example, to have a bureaucracy, and the question of how power is exercised in such a Church is a question (and challenge) to the bureaucracy as much as the public office-holders. The precondition for understanding how various powers work within the Church is a willingness to be open to analysis. Concealment or denial is a way of adopting the disguises of invulnerability.

One of the resources referred to earlier in the chapter, the *Pastoral Rule* of Gregory the Great, contains a remarkable example of the benefits of recognizing that the Church is involved in the distribution and exercise of ordinary, 'secular' power. Gregory's treatise is addressed to people he calls 'rulers or rectors – *rectores*', and these are both bishops and prominent lay people. As a consequence of his view that bishops have such powers, he writes vividly about, and with great psychological insight into, the danger of becoming conceited. He is absolutely insistent on a radical theological egalitarianism – we all share a common fallen nature. Those who exercise power in the Church need to protect themselves from pride by vigorous self-examination and by the exercise of disciplined humility. But at the same time the fact that *rectores* can also be lay people in positions of leadership entails the application to them of the same principles of humility in greatness. This is why what we call the 'service ethic' has played such a role in Christian civilization. It also explains why Machiavelli's onslaught on the idea of altruism in political power transactions was so shocking to sixteenth-century Christian thought.

Christians ought, however, to resist the temptation to hand over the concept of power, lock, stock and barrel, to amoral so-called 'realists'. Apart from the consequences for the theory and practice of politics, this would also have the effect of making aspects of the life of the Church quite unintelligible. Anonymity in the exercise of power is in principle more dangerous and corrupting than the open acknowledgement of it. Those who do as a matter of fact exercise power in the Church need to know that they do so, if they are to be as aware as they should be of the need for great spiritual discipline.

In the modern Church of England powers are distributed in internally complex ways. They reside both in office-holders and in bureaucrats, in the ordained and in lay people serving on synods. And because the Church has its own unique goals and values particular kinds of giftedness, saintliness has its own special kind of influence irrespective of formal public roles. The Christian understanding of power which we have been expounding brings it much closer to home and makes it more ordinary and familiar, than the negative, looming and threatening concept it has become in modern society. The gift to every Christian of the Holy Spirit, bearing a unique gift to be used for the building-up and empowerment of the whole Church, is a gift of power. It is a gift to be recognized and used, not to be hidden or denied. With it may come temptations of various kinds – even the fact that it is appreciated and valued by others in the Church may become, as Gregory the Great devastatingly makes clear, a source of pride. No one, therefore, should regard themselves as exempt from the disciplines of humility. It is very striking that in a passage in 1 Peter, where the writer is expounding the leadership tasks of 'elders' and the necessity that 'younger' people be subordinate to them, he insists that humility is mutual and reciprocal;

'all of you [he says] must clothe yourselves with humility in your dealings with one other' (1 Peter 5.5).

In the reported dispute between the disciples, Jesus' rebuke is accompanied by the instruction that 'the greatest among you must become like the youngest' (Luke 22.26); or that 'whoever wishes to become great among you must be your servant' (Mark 10.43). The example of greatness and at the same time of service, of being the highest and yet a servant, is his own. The exercise of power is thus not presented as an alternative to service, but as an essential means of service. From the rest of the accounts of Jesus' ministry in the Gospels, it is apparent that Jesus uses his powers in response to human needs, and that in his teaching he invites but does not compel response. The words, 'Come to me, all you that are weary and are carrying heavy burdens, and I will give you rest' (Matthew 11.28), contain this tone of service in greatness.

As fallible human beings we can easily make serious mistakes about the methods we use in discipleship of Christ, even when professing our service of God's reign and sovereignty. It is for this reason that those who seek to use God-given powers in the struggle against evil have to remain open to admonition about what we have done and the way in which we have done it. No human being is exempt from error. The rich and powerful are not in the right because of their resources and status; the poor are not in the right because of their lack of resources and status. Admonition is mutual. But the temptation of the rich is always to use their resources to establish immunity from criticism and to stifle debate, rather than as a means of including those who are marginalized.

Here again Gregory the Great is quite explicit, and uses the biblical examples of Paul rebuking Peter (Galatians 2.11), and of Nathan rebuking David (2 Samuel 12.7). Good rulers, he adds, should be humble enough to take such blunt admonitions as a compliment to their humility. At the same time Gregory is utterly realistic about the implications of such freedoms, which have their own attached responsibilities. The critics are not invariably right or even fair in their criticisms, one might observe. But protecting their right to be critical is part of a properly disciplined exercise of power.

Because all human beings are made in God's image and likeness and are all alike accountable to God at the last judgement, the task of all who acknowledge God's sovereignty is to promote and enable as radical a degree of inclusivity as possible. Social processes always have a chronic tendency to marginalize or exclude certain unfavoured categories of people, usually in the interests of dominant majorities. In Jesus' day the marginal included people suffering from certain sorts of illness, including lepers and the insane. The purity laws tended to make certain occupations unacceptable, and other races unclean. Jesus' teaching and social practice revolutionized these traditions, and the implications of it went on reverberating after his death and resurrection. The inclusion of all people within the scope of God's new covenant, together with their final accountability to God, made of Christianity a universal faith with a powerful urge both to speak of God's love for all humankind, and to practise that inclusive love within human society. The restoration of God's image is a process rightly understood as empowerment, a transformation of the multiple weaknesses of humankind completed in God's own time.

Conclusion

The forming of what we have called a 'truthful moral imagination' in relation to the powers we exercise as human beings is not a simple matter. We cannot extract ourselves from the network of powers which influence us, and in relation to which we are able to make significant decisions. Wisdom in our exercises of power is not easily won. Those in positions of power are liable to be biased in judging their own case. Those who are comparatively powerless are prone to assume the role of victims. All of us are acutely subject to self-deception.

As we have seen, Christian theology involves an understanding of the power of God; but at the same time it is not a kind of power about which one can make easy assumptions. Living in the context of the story of God's power, of God's love for creation and humankind, of God's grace and generosity in humbling himself, of God's decision to dwell with the humble in heart, and of God's empowering of all who seek him, is a shaping of our limited powers into the pathway of wisdom.

In western politics and philosophy 'power' has come to have formidably negative connotations, and suspicion is now in-built in our attitude to those who exercise it in public. Politicians and journalists – it is no accident – are the least trusted persons in modern society. Our survey has illustrated part of the reason why this has come about, and it is clear that the Scriptures themselves understand the potential for abuse in the power exercised in both society and the Church.

But the return to our sources reminds us that in the Christian view power cannot be seen as intrinsically corrupt. To be created by God entails being gifted with human powers, the wise use of which is integral to being fully human. To be redeemed by God entails living in the light of the power of the Resurrection. To be sanctified by God entails enjoyment and exercise of the gifts of the Holy Spirit. In all the ordinary ways in which it is open to any of God's creatures to exercise their powers, it is also open to live extraordinarily, drawn by the power of God and never separated from it.

> His divine power has given us everything needed for life and godliness, through the knowledge of him who called us by his own glory and goodness. Thus he has given us, through these things, his precious and very great promises, so that through them you may escape from the corruption that is in the world because of lust, and may become participants of the divine nature. (2 Peter 1.3-4)

Chapter 4
Money

Why include money?

Is money essential to being human?

Money might seem a most unlikely candidate for inclusion as a central theme in a discussion of what it means to be human. Perhaps it is even more strikingly odd when included in a report that aims to articulate what it means to be human beings before God.

Money might not seem to be an essential and defining aspect of human nature. We know after all that there have been societies, groups and individuals who have lived without money, and that some such societies still exist; they are certainly no less human. Money seems more an accidental feature of developed human society, not an essential aspect of human nature or of our relationship to God. Money is not like time, then, not an inescapable aspect of humanity. So why should it be given any more consideration by those working on a Christian understanding of our humanity than, say, football or automatic washing machines?

So it is true that money is an accidental, rather than an essential in respect of our humanity. Whilst other animals have not developed symbolic media for the exchange of commodities, it would be hard to make the case that our having done so is what defines or constitutes us as human beings. But, at this point in human cultural and social development, money is almost universal, and necessarily so. It cannot be avoided. We are obliged to be involved with money, simply in order to transact our lives. Life, in all its abundant possibilities, is unthinkable – more importantly, unliveable – without it. In a complex society such as ours, it is simply not possible to pursue self-sufficiency to the point where one never becomes involved with money. A life without money would lack much of the diversity and richness that the development of money has made possible. Some of the institutions on which we most depend, the National Health Service to take an obvious example, are inconceivable without our being able to pay for them in money.

So whilst in the abstract money may not seem to be part of what defines, it most certainly is a vital aspect of the world in which we *actually* live and work out our humanity. If we want to understand humanity before God as lived out in the realities of our world, then it is necessary to pay attention both to what money is and how we relate to it. In what follows, we shall suggest that money is not only part of the structure of the human world in which we actually live, but that it exerts great power to structure and shape our humanity as we live in a world constituted in part by money. In that sense at least, money is part of what gives concrete shape to our lived humanity. (To anticipate what will come later: speaking of money in this way may alert us to the fact that we are more used to thinking of money as something we do things with, not as something that may do something to us and to the world.)

Wealth or money?

A second reason this focus on money may seem odd is that it has so seldom been given direct attention in Bible, tradition or subsequent doctrinal discussion. It is very much more common to find discussion of the spiritual and theological dangers of *wealth* than those posed by money itself. Of course, wealth can mean (and, in biblical times, usually would have meant) the accumulation of land, goods or precious metals; wealth need not necessarily be held in money. There is thus strong encouragement from Bible and tradition to regard wealth as the primary, theologically significant, topic and to relegate the treatment of money as secondary to that.

Wealth is without doubt an extremely important theme in the living of a Christian life. But discussing wealth draws attention towards certain forms of (more or less deliberate, more or less individual) behaviour with money and away from the nature and behaviour of money. We wish to concentrate on money, without being drawn immediately into a discussion of wealth, because we consider the shaping power of money *as money* to be significant, regardless of whether we have or are pursuing wealth. Moreover, treating money as a synonym for wealth associates the theological and spiritual danger of money not with the nature and behaviour of money itself, but with responses and attitudes (greed and fear, say) that prompt us to seek the supposed security of accumulating it. So while declaring money neutral we can easily make it the subject of theological discussion only when our behaviour towards it becomes pathological or sinful. Whilst we shall sound a critical and cautionary note concerning the specific system of money that operates globally today, what we hope to achieve in drawing direct attention to it is to give it balanced but positive affirmation as a theological topic.

It is because money is regarded as external to human nature rather than essential to it that it is more usually discussed as wealth, and dealt with as a theme of ethics rather than doctrine. So attention tends to be given not to money in itself, but to our *attitude* towards and *behaviour* with money, to avarice, possessions, economic justice, wealth, and poverty, questions of social and political discipleship, whereas it is something of a novelty to find money discussed at all in works of Christian doctrine. This might easily be taken to suggest that money is a theological or spiritual issue only at the level of behaviour and attitude, not in itself.

On the face of it, the Bible speaks much more frequently about individual and corporate *behaviour* in relation to money than about money itself. We can find passages without difficulty that deal with wealth, poverty, greed, debt, economic justice and possessions. There are far fewer that talk about money as such. Indeed, when we do find attention turned towards money we can find such interpretation reinforced that money is an instrument, like an axe good in itself but capable of misuse when we use it to lop our neighbour's head off. Preachers often point out that it is a misquotation of the Bible to present it as condemning money as the root of all evil. It is not money, but the *love* of money that is condemned (1 Timothy 6.10). So it has generally been assumed that we should talk about our *attitudes* to and *use* of money. Money is not the problem (and there is no need to discuss it if it is not a problem): we are the problem. It is not money that defines us theologically or spiritually, but our personal attitudes, orientations and desires – including those relating to money – rooted deeply in and definitive of our selves.

Hence, it is more usual to look inward to inspect the constellation of our desires to explain both pathologies and virtues in our handling of money, and not to money itself. This supposes that our desires and personal attitudes are established and shaped quite apart from our exposure to and involvement with money. Whilst it might be admitted that wealth and poverty have some shaping effect on identity and on the patterning of desire, these do not relate to the character of money itself. Money is generally regarded as neutral. We wish in what follows to put forward a rather different view, one that sees money as a good, though one that has immense power to shape identity and desire.

We certainly wish to affirm that money is a human good and an essential instrument for any imaginable human society which aims at human flourishing. We also wish to affirm the strong strand of biblical and traditional teaching that our attitudes towards money are indicative of our spirituality. But we wish at the same time to affirm that the nature and function of money itself, as a profound influence shaping us as human beings, needs careful theological investigation. We are clear that money is far from being a simple and neutral reality which we can take at its face value and easily control its part in shaping our lives. Believing that money and the financial system under which we live are good and a tribute to human ingenuity does not mean we can remain innocent about what money is actually doing to us, even if we claim not to 'love' it.

Our money

More than notes and coins

What is money? The answer to this question appears obvious: notes and coins are, of course, money. But pointing to these objects would be a quite inadequate answer to the question, 'What is money?' Notes and coins are money, but they are not what money is (indeed, increasingly money exchanges involve no issued currency at all, but the transfer of figures from one account to another). 'Money' is much more like a verb than a noun; it names activity or function rather than a set of discrete objects in the world. Money is dynamic; it is activity; it is function. What makes notes and coins money is not some quality or intrinsic property they have in themselves, but the functions they perform in human society (even more clearly now that there is no relationship between currency and precious metals). For the notes and coins (and the figures on the accounts) to function as money requires a set of social, cultural and political, as well as economic, arrangements. Money is a human and social reality, not something that can be abstracted from specific human contexts. This is not the place to lay out the history of money in all its fine detail, but human societies and their monetary instruments have evolved together. Whilst there are some general properties that are basic to the definition and application of the term, the nature and function of money are not constant but change through time and with social, cultural, economic and societal contexts.

One reason why it is not possible simply to 'read off' what the Bible says about money and apply it to our own situation is that money differs markedly in its nature and function between biblical times and our own day. Indeed, part of that difference lies in how very much less significant money was to economic life then. In those days there simply was much less money in circulation. The result was not merely that society was relatively less wealthy; money did not perform the central role in economic life that it does in our society. Other means of exchange were more frequently used and wealth or poverty were related primarily not to possession of money, but of land. By contrast, in our case there are few aspects of modern life that are imaginable, much less navigable, without it.

The relatively recent but extraordinarily far-reaching changes in the nature and function of money make it even more important to avoid abstraction and the suggestion that money is a simple, straightforward and univocal term and reality. It is these developments that also make it necessary to focus clearly on money in this discussion rather than wealth. For unless we recognize that recent developments in the system of money place us in a new situation, we shall either approach it in a superficial way with little theological reflection, or we shall apply outdated modes of analysis. In the following section, some of the most significant recent developments are sketched.

Money as unit of exchange value

The most obvious function of money is to express the relative value of goods and services so that trade and exchange may be transacted without recourse to direct barter. The invention and use of money represents a human good, which enabled the development and flourishing of human communities through productivity, trade and the specialization and division of both labour and production. Money allows a great deal of creativity to be focused and energized that would not have been possible in a system of trade reliant on barter. Initially, weighed-out ingots (later pressed coins) of precious metal, in which there was a market, and so an established (and relatively stable) market price (value), were used. That had happened by biblical times, when the common unit of exchange was units of weight of the precious metals used for coins. For that reason, alongside the survival of barter for some transactions, wealth would also have been held in and trade conducted through the exchange of the items made out of precious metals and stones as well as that crafted specifically to be money.

Today, coins are minted out of base and cheap metals; notes out of paper. But the physical circulation of currency now accounts for only a small proportion of transactions. Most take place as the increasingly rapid electronic transfer of figures from one account to another. In neither case is their monetary value related to what they are made of. But since before the Second World War, neither does their value relate to the issuing nation's holdings of precious metal. The link to a standard of value external to the financial system has disappeared. To understand the current significance of this, it is first necessary to appreciate a medieval development: credit.

Credit

Around the twelfth century in Europe, money took on an additional asset function, which represents a significant and qualitative change with the development of credit. This made possible the development of modern banking and financial systems and allowed the lending of money to those with a need for it (often for capital investment projects) held by those whose holdings were surplus to their own immediate requirements. Hence, the assets of those who could not presently capitalize on them (or did not wish to risk to) could be temporarily transferred to those who could. This development allowed the much more effective use of a society's wealth and resources and led directly to increased prosperity of modern European societies. The asset function of money released through credit should therefore be considered a good that can serve human flourishing.

As well as borrowing other people's money, the creation of credit made two other things possible. First, it enabled borrowing not only against the wealth accumulated by another but also against one's projected *future* wealth. Second, the development of 'fractional reserve banking' permitted the lending by banks of statutorily regulated multiples of the deposits received from investors and savers. That is to say, the deposits they held were a 'fractional reserve' of the amount they actually lent. This greatly increased the amount of money they could lend, and has made banks effectively into creators of money.

These developments in credit creation, together with the erosion of reference to a reality outside the money system, means that money depends now more than at any other time on trust. The character of that trust has also changed. No longer does it represent confidence that the value of money is backed either by holdings of precious metal or the level of wealth subsisting in the level of economic activity in the economy as a whole. Now there is no reference to a hard, external reality. All depends on the confidence that others will not insist on withdrawing their deposits and will continue themselves to have trust and confidence in the value of their and our money.

This is a highly significant development, which since the Second World War has made the supply of money a matter of decision, regulation and planning. The amount of money in circulation need not now bear any direct relation to a pot of accumulated wealth that underwrites it. The amount of money in circulation can be adjusted in order to effect adjustments in the level of activity within an economy. However, the last forty years have seen further developments along these lines, which potentially threaten that confidence, and have given rise to movements to rein back the quantity and power of money. For as the supply of money grew (principally following rises in the price of oil), so 'fractional reserve banking' meant that the amount of money being lent grew exponentially, with consequences in international indebtedness and consumer credit that are now well known. Added to that, the development of electronic means of transmitting money means that it circulates much faster. All this means that money, while remaining a human good, has acquired a dominance in our society which must raise severe questions about its potential power to shape human life in destructive as well as constructive ways.

A market in money

In its origin money bore a fairly direct relation to the realities of human productivity and trade. Generally restricted in use to a specific community, it could perform a unitive function for that community in its producing and trading of goods and services. (Of course, money has been used to oppress and to serve selfish ends that work against the flourishing of the whole community; we are not reading that history through rosy spectacles.) But with the break of the link between money and real wealth-production, with the instruments of credit creation (i.e. the instrument through which money may be increased vastly beyond the level of deposits held), globalization and the technology permitting the transfer of money at the speed of light, the conditions were met for the creation of a market for instant trade in money as a commodity itself.

Both the fact and the actual working of the market in money has changed the nature of money. In excess of 90 per cent of the worth of transactions do not relate to productivity in the real world at all, but represent speculations about the future value of a specific currency (and by extension, of the valuation – as distinct from the real worth and value – of the economy and of the society that transacts its life through that economy). Money almost entirely freed from a relationship to the value of goods and services in the lives of human beings and their communities has, in effect, been removed from the sphere of human values. Its growth and movement seek the optimization, not of the conditions for human flourishing (or even of wealth creation through production, provision of services or trade), but of its own power to reproduce more of itself. The market in money follows its own laws, oriented on increasing the monetary value of investors' holdings of money – as though money were, not only the arbiter of the worth of everything else, but a good and an end in itself, self-validating and self-legitimating. Money has taken on a life of its own.

What is traded on is no longer the actual worth of productive activity within an economy (and thereby the real, backed strength of that economy), but the relative levels of confidence of other investors and speculators in the currency – only very loosely and indirectly (and not necessarily) related to its actual strength and vitality, much less to the human values it may or may not be serving. Whilst the relationship to the external realities of economic activity in the economy have been broken in one direction (from production and trade to currency: the backing of currency), they remain strong in the other. Confidence in the currency may be entirely unrelated to the worth of what is being conducted within it, but the speculative decisions made on the basis of such confidence (and the perceptions of others' future confidence and the decisions they will make) can and do determine the 'value' of one currency against another in ways that severely impact on the real world economy and the human beings that live within it.

Because more money is chasing goods and services, and because money is in principle insatiable in its demands, an economy and culture centred on money is prone to anxiety. Money will never arrive at a point where it is capable of being sated, of saying 'enough'. Whilst the expansion of credit means that money no longer symbolizes and represents stored wealth, it nonetheless represents a stored potential claim against the world's resources. And because the supply of money is ever-expanding, these claims and the monetary power to pursue them likewise expand and consequentially distort markets based in some more direct relationship to human need or sufficiency.

Money and us

Supposed objectivity

As a common, *mathematical*, unit of valuation, money presents itself as neutral in its operation and as indicating the 'objective' or 'true' worth of things. The relative value of everything may be quantified and it is tempting to suppose that this exchange value represents real human or intrinsic worth. But what determines exchange values is seldom real intrinsic worth, but the price that can be fetched in 'the market'. That in turn is determined by the level of demand and by the intensity of that demand, which relates not only to 'need' (which just might reflect intrinsic worth) but to the economic power of those making the demand.

Furthermore, since money is a numerical reality, and our dealings in, with and through it are worked out through the universal truths and laws of mathematics, it easily presents its performance as a realm of necessity. One cannot question the operation and effects of money any more than one may question the truth of the principles of mathematics it invokes or the law of gravity.

This is intensified by the move of money away from a reference to the intrinsic (or at least the exchange) value of goods and services.

Disembodied and disembedded figures and their mathematical interrelation have become primary as the trade in money has taken precedence in value (and arguably therefore in economic significance) over that in tangible goods and services and where that trade is also conducted through transfer of figures rather than exchange of physical currency. Mathematical units and values come to be believed in practice as more real than tangible items that are produced and traded; as, indeed, the arbiters of the worth of everything else. The way in which value is constructed is reversed. What once functioned primarily as a quantitative measure of the qualities and value of things in the world and of the work and worth of human beings now easily turns into the primary referent of their quality. That which money once valued is now increasingly valued only in relation to what has become the primary and apparently objective quality in relation to which all else is measured, and that is money.

This is as true of people's ability to command monetary wealth (wages, benefits, but also credit-worthiness). Our value and worth are equated with our participation in the system of money and the way in which it rewards us. For this reason also money becomes the measure of worth in our key institutions and financial disciplines are used to regulate them as though other values were irrelevant. When building societies were permitted to turn themselves into banks, the resulting bonuses appeared as windfalls that had cost nobody anything, when in fact they were the result of the productive activity of earlier generations. So money can appear to grow by magic, without any relevance to to whether or not it is serving human flourishing.

The explosion of credit

Fractional reserve banking does not only create credit for the use of capital investors and their like. It does so at the centre of the everyday economic activity of ordinary people. The last twenty years have seen a massive increase in the amount of credit available and used in our economy by all income groups, on credit cards, consumer credit in the high street and in mortgage borrowing (against vastly increased home prices). It has also seen the introduction of the Social Fund for the poorest members of our society, which extends credit to them for the purchase of essentials, and of the system of student loans to fund university-level education. Above all, there has been a substantial increase in money supply through easily obtainable consumer credit to fuel the ever more avid consumption of consumer goods.

Credit has become central to the way that we manage and live our lives. One of the ways in which it has become culturally acceptable to live by borrowing heavily against anticipated future earnings is to term it 'credit' rather than 'debt'. We tend to assume that those of us who do not borrow beyond our actual ability to repay do not have 'debt' and are not adversely affected by our behaviour with money.

We also notice that credit can make things possible for people that were not possible before, and we are bound to consider it only fair that a far wider cross-section of the population than before has access to credit – even if, for the poorest, that can often be at a very high rate of interest. The opportunity of home ownership with the aid of a mortgage is a very good example of the way this expansion of credit can offer a sense of liberation to many people, while also bringing in its train difficulties that may not be obvious at first.

In Britain, for all sorts of good reasons, there is a long tradition of home ownership, even if for much of our history that could only be a pipe dream for many. Now it is not, largely because of the recent changes in credit creation (specifically, the increased availability of mortgages), and a much higher percentage of Britons 'own' their own home than is true of any other European nation. But what has happened to mortgages serves as a good example of the effects on prices of increases in the supply of money (effectively a devaluation in the value of money against a specific good). (At the same time, we are tempted to see the increasing value of our homes as an increase in their intrinsic worth.) As house prices increase (especially for those entering the market unable to capitalize on the increased monetary asset value of a previous home), so does the size of mortgages. More significantly, both in relation to income and to other expenditure, the servicing of mortgage debt has increased dramatically.

When the repayment of the interest on our debts form such a significant proportion of our income, our lives become centred in practice around service of that debt; our future becomes mortgaged and our relationship to time is fundamentally reconfigured – though we may be quite unaware of it. For this is not necessarily a process of conscious elevation of value. That is because what we actually take *in practice* to be of ultimate value and worth can go unrecognized and may even stand in direct contradiction to the way in which we are consciously steering and trying to give shape to our lives. The need to service debt is generally a demand that we meet first as a strict necessity of life, with no more reflection on it, or awareness that it might be the base value of our lives than we give to breathing air. Significantly, when interest rates are stable, most people's repayments require no conscious activity. They go from our accounts and never feature in the pot of disposable income about which we make decisions. Mortgage repayment appears to us to be necessary and so to be value-free, not something we have choice about. So they also appear spiritually and theologically neutral – not our entrance into a highly charged spiritual dynamic. It is so basic to the pattern of existence that it becomes an unquestioning assumption, and we pattern life around it. We think of values as related to choices we make, and may therefore by quite unaware of how activities and attitudes that seem just natural and necessary may be shaping our deepest perceptions and desires.

What is true for us as individuals is also true for us as citizens. It is a largely unchallenged assumption that borrowing money in the market – or from the 'private sector' – is the only satisfactory way to finance major developments in public services such as hospitals. While the propriety of 'private finance initiatives' is a matter about which there is a good deal of debate, and the arguments will vary in strength according to particular circumstances, of one thing there is no doubt: the servicing of the debt so incurred will inevitably come in times of economic difficulty to take precedence over those for whom the service is being provided (patients or pupils) since otherwise the money will not be lent in the first place. Thus, without acknowledgement, money and its rewards predominate.

Money and community

Money is a common unit of valuation, and such can only be secured by social agreement. Hence, when we talk about money, we are not talking about a set of *financial* relationships pertaining in some sphere detached from *social* relationships, but a particular mode of material and social relationship between human beings. Money requires society and social consensus, though not necessarily enjoying conscious and explicit consent. Where these are not already in place, it can build them as it facilitates and shapes the material and social relationships between human beings. Money is dependent on and brings human beings into *material* relationships of exchange with one another.

We are perhaps so used to thinking of money as facilitating transactions, as the exchange of goods and services, that we may easily become inattentive to the fact that such transactions are generally between human beings. Indeed, it is likely that the origin of money lies in the elevation in value of certain artefacts or natural phenomena in social exchanges between human beings. Significant human relationships or events would be marked and furthered by the exchange of tokens (beads, teeth, gold, shells, animals), which later came to be used in commercial transactions in view of the social value already accorded them. The origin of money lies primarily in the exchange of gifts to foster human relationships. Its use in commerce was a subsequent development out of that. When we use money to engage in a financial transaction, human beings are still being brought into specific ways of relating to one another, and we would do well to remember that. The question is: what sort of relationship do money transactions facilitate in any given society and financial system and in specific cases?

The use of money in facilitating transactions between people may facilitate a certain mode or form of relationship between them; it may embed or change the kind of relationship that exists between them already; but moneyed transactions may also bring people into certain kinds of relationship who were not in relationship before. Money may be the instrument of establishing relationship (say, between people at great geographical distances through vast commodity markets) and of establishing the possibility of this particular kind of relationship (say, that between producer and manufacturer and consumer), even where the people may have had other modes of relationship in place already.

Yet, because money does not require direct exchange between producers or providers on the one hand and consumers on the other, it facilitates a far more complex set of relationships and exchanges than would have been possible through, say, a system of barter. Of particular significance is the fact that, through money, people can be brought into relationships that are transacted across great distances and may well be anonymous too. So much that has been creative in our life as community has been made possible by the developments in money that we need to remind ourselves also of another side: that money can devastate relationships, lending money can ruin friendships, and the prospect of winning huge sums of money through the National Lottery, for example, can distort lives beyond recognition. There is more to money than the figures that dance before our eyes.

Money and desire: some unconventional assumptions

As we said at the outset of this chapter, we have traditionally located concern with our *attitudes* to money rather than with money itself. That 'rather than' powerfully suggests a sharp dichotomy between what is supposedly internal to the person and what external; between, on the one hand, the spirituality shaping desire and the external objects for which one may have inappropriate desire; between one's love of money and money itself. It suggests that money is seen as an external object of choice, outside the person. It is seen as a neutral tool or instrument, of functional utility in the pursuit of other desires. Though we acknowledge that this tool may also become the object and end of our desires, this too may be seen in terms of the free decision of a self, whose desire for money is constituted and shaped independently of the reality of and relationship with money; independently, that is, of what money actually and in practice is. That is why we are tempted to regard internal attitudes and spiritual orientation (including towards money) as significant in defining our humanity, and not those realities we choose as objects of our desire.

Indeed, this is why it might seem odd to find money included in a theological consideration of humanity. We think of money as notes and coins, as a tool, or else as a possible object of desire amongst others that we may *freely* choose to pursue or not. The desires we fulfil through use of money, and even our love of and desire for money itself, are expressive of our spirit and its fundamental orientations in the world. But are we right to assume that our spirit and its desires are self-constituting, shaped in some neutral sphere, expressive of a self and its desires already shaped and constituted apart from its relationship to money? Are we right to assume that we are free in relation to money, free to choose whether and how we associate our lives with it and what meaning it shall have for us? Are we right to assume that money is more like a substance (a tool or an object) than a field of force, an activity or a network of relationships? Are we right and is it safe to assume that money exerts no power? Are we right to assume that we use money instrumentally, to meet our needs and desires, without money itself shaping our needs and desires, our sense of what is good, right and true? Above all, are we right to assume that the kind of problem that money can be is fundamentally a personal one, a matter of our private, internal, moral or spiritual values and orientation? Moreover, are we right to treat these as uninvolved with and unshaped by the social dynamics and structures (including financial and economic ones) within which we live? Are problems with money, in essence, simply those of individual moral and spiritual failures, which express already-established pathologies of the self?

The first clue from the tradition that such assumptions might be unsafe comes simply from the frequency with which our actual involvement with money is proclaimed to be spiritually dangerous. The frequency with which human beings' actual involvement with money is seen in the Bible to be problematic suggests that we should be wary of taking comfort in the status of money as a necessary and taken-for-granted good. Perhaps this is related to the fact that Bible and tradition rarely deal with money in the abstract, as an idea or a concept, but as a reality in a particular social world; that is, within a nexus of actual human relationships within a specific social and economic ordering of human affairs. Does it suggest that there is something about money in the real world, rather than in the abstract, that is problematic? Is there, after all, something about our involvement with money that is less like possession or use of an object and more like a highly charged spiritual dynamic or force? That our use of money does not only give rise to issues that can be adequately handled through the (secularized?) language of ethics, but is a significant spiritual and theological issue? It would then not only be a matter for individuals of regulating their external behaviour, but of securing justice.

The second clue comes from the preponderance of texts, especially in the Old Testament, where consideration of the pathologies of money (gross poverty, unequal distribution of wealth and, in particular, of its base in land, injustice, etc.) do not concern themselves exclusively with questions of individual decision-making. Rather, questions of personal morality and spirituality are addressed in the context of broader socially institutionalized economic arrangements in which money has some kind of power. These suggest that money does not only have power over us when we freely choose to relate to it in specific ways that reflect some individual personal pathology on our part. Money also has power by virtue of what it is and how it functions in the order of a particular society – power for good, but also power for ill.

This belief in our inner freedom to mould our own desires about money, tempting though it is, is also challenged in our own experience. Can anyone believe that the increased availability of credit does not at the same time change our moral sense about whether it is good or bad to be in debt? Does not the frequency with which we see huge prizes awarded as the random outcome of a gamble and huge rewards given to those at the head of organizations (even failing ones) affect how far money starts to glitter before us, enticing us with its capacity to procure what we want and calm our fears of finding ourselves destitute and in need? These are rhetorical questions; the evidence of those we know, let alone the evidence of research into such topics as student indebtedness, gives a very clear answer: the human will is shaped by that with which human beings occupy themselves every day and the assumptions they find themselves making.

Flourishing

In the Bible, we find discussion of wealth and money – all economic activity – contextualized within the whole purposes of God that calls and constitutes the community.

So Jubilee (cf. Leviticus 25) is not concerned primarily with the redistribution of money, since money was far less significant than was ownership of the land. Significantly, the control of debt is a major concern. The intention may easily be applied to an economic system like our own, since the overall theme is to ensure that economic systems are interrupted and so do not acquire a life of their own to the extent that they disorient people from the divine purpose and calling. Hence, the biblical idea of Jubilee does not address money at all, but insists that land, as the basis of the community's wealth, belongs to the whole community. The purpose of economic life does not relate primarily to the perceived good of those who may capitalize on it in some way; rather, it is for the flourishing of the community. Economic life is thus subordinated to the human flourishing in the covenant community. The debt accrued over the history of financial and economic transactions is not therefore allowed to accrue in an unchecked way that fundamentally and in perpetuity alters people's relationship to the basic means of their survival – the land given to the community by God and held in trust as part of the covenant gift – and, indeed, fundamentally alters and undermines the dynamics of the community itself.

Community and concern for the destitute is very strong in the Bible. What is the significance of that? One inference that might be drawn is that any treatment of money or wealth has to include, and arguably should begin with, the perspective of those who are on the economic underside. We should take care, however, in assuming consonance between terms such as 'the poor' as used in the Bible and in our own context. What the Bible means by 'the poor' differs somewhat from what we might usually mean by the term. The poor are not the 'less wealthy', those who have sufficient economic resources for survival, but perhaps not much more and considerably less than the rich or the averagely wealthy. In the world of the Bible, that group would be large and made up of many peasants and artisans – those who had the means to make a living at around the subsistence level. Poverty in the Bible, however, is synonymous with actual or virtual destitution, as the opening of this paragraph itself indicates. 'The poor' means in the Bible those who lack economic security, living dangerously on the edge of destitution, or those who are destitute, who cannot survive except by begging or crime or selling themselves into slavery. Often the category is extended a little to include those who are very vulnerable economically: widows, orphans, resident aliens (sojourners), and day labourers (for example, Exodus 22.21-22; Job 24.3-4; Zechariah 7.9-10; Mark 12.41-44; James 1.27) and also disabled people (Leviticus 19.14; Luke 4.18).

In these terms, wealth and poverty in the Old Testament are intimately connected with power and social status. The poor are powerless, unable to protect their rights and interests against those with social power. The rich had the social good of honour, even if regarded as oppressors, while the poor tended to be despised (as we can tell from injunctions not to do so, e.g., Proverbs 14.31; 17.5). Furthermore, there is a strong association in the Bible between money-derived power, privilege, status and arrogance, which appears to be a resistance to the 'economy' of grace and gift. Money was one of the means whereby the rich could store up this security and power ('riches' would be the other), of relying on it and living from this security, instead of from the gift of God. The economy of self-securing, of attachment, substitutes for that of living from the abundance of life given by God; of a life in, through and towards God.

One fact of far-reaching significance about the difference between such ancient societies and our own is the absence of the two interdependent assumptions and expectations of a modern economy: that individuals shall constantly improve their standard of living and that the economy is expected to grow without limit. The Old Testament's classic picture of utopian existence – everyone under their own fig tree (1 Kings 4.25; Micah 4.4; etc.) – is simply the life of the ordinary peasant family at its best: owning their own modest smallholding, producing enough to live and with leisure enough to enjoy it, and with no threat from the rapacious rich or foreign invasion. Even when imagining the idyllic future, Israelite peasants wanted no more than this in material terms.

People who wanted to make money beyond ordinary sufficiency were greedy and warned of the folly (e.g. Proverbs 23.4-5) or the consequences of gaining wealth. It was generally thought obvious that the rich could be rich only at the expense of the poor, that the economy had a 'zero-sum' in which the gains of some could only be achieved at the expense of others, and furthermore of others who would live in close proximity and know one another, as the rich man of whom Jesus spoke knew Lazarus who begged at his own gate.

Both the legislation of the Torah and the oracles of the prophets presuppose a shared notion of what the society of God's covenant people should be like. Each family owns its own smallholding, which passes down in the ownership of the family inalienably. That inalienability of a family's right to its land was based on God's gift of the land to all his people. No doubt there was never any thought of strict, mathematical equality between families, but any accumulation of land was recognized as being at the expense of others. Therefore, the prophets condemn those who add field to field, and the Torah has a great deal of legislation designed to prevent accumulation of wealth by some and the impoverishment of others. Making money out of money (usury) is forbidden. Sabbatical and Jubilee years ensure release from debt and slavery and the return of land to its original owners.

It is in relation to this sense of the material conditions that attend the flourishing of the community that the linking of God's blessing with prosperity should be read. Prosperity does not mean surplus wealth, but refers to things such as the weather conditions to ensure good harvests. The expectation is that the peasant family will live quite well from their smallholding, not that they will use the surplus to accumulate wealth and land. In general, the Torah legislates against there being rich people, the prophets denounce the political and economic developments which produced a significant class of rich landowners and wealthy bureaucrats, the psalmists complain to God against their oppression by the rich, wisdom considers the pursuit of wealth foolish. There are different approaches to wealth in the Old Testament, but not much comfort for the rich.

The legal and moral frameworks developed in response to the covenant which binds God's people together impel the community to make provision for the poor (those without land, who cannot work and have no relatives to provide for them).

The association of wealth with problematic spirituality in the Old Testament has been widely rehearsed. For that reason, and because it addresses more squarely the issue of wealth rather than money, we shall say very little about it here. The poor, destitute of worldly goods, come to represent the paradigm of proper reliance on God. The rich, on the other hand, become paradigmatic of a heart hardened at once against the plight of the poor whom they exploit (or at least could help) and arrogant and proud, assured in their self-reliance, in relation to God.

If we see Jesus' ministry as aimed at the eschatological renewal of God's people Israel in the dawning rule of God, then we can see Jesus as implementing the imperatives of the Torah, the prophets and the wise in relation to the poor in typically radical forms. He goes out of his way to bring into the sphere of God's grace the destitute and marginalized of all kinds, including disabled beggars, demoniacs, lepers, prostitutes and (reminding us that economic status was not his only criterion of marginality) rich tax collectors and the chronically sick in wealthy families. And who does he make paradigmatic for his disciples, already living out God's rule? The poor, children, day labourers, beggars and slaves. Jesus reconstitutes society under God's rule by making people with no or extremely low status and no privilege the paradigm to which others must conform. It was not impossible for the rich to enter the kingdom and live by its values, but it was difficult, since it demanded going beyond generosity or charity towards the destitute. It meant abandoning the arrogance of privilege in order to treat them as equals and enter into community with them. The reversal of status practised by Jesus finds its echoes throughout the rest of the New Testament and in the practice of the early Christian community (e.g. 1 Corinthians 1.26-29; James 1.9-11).

Being human before God with money

Choices we have, and choices we do not have

The human race has no choice about whether or not to live with money. Those societies and parts of societies where money has very little place may continue to use other media of exchange for as long as they are able to remain outside the operation of the global market – which we may judge will not be very long and certainly not for ever. Those in our society who have very little money will in many cases continue to find other ways of mutual support and generosity and will perforce live lives in which money plays only a small part, because they only have a small amount of it. But for the most part and for nearly all human beings money is a reality of their lives and will continue to be so. It represents, as we have affirmed, a triumph of human ingenuity that has made possible social developments of enormous significance; it has put down deep roots in nearly all cultures over millennia; its development is a sign of continuing human ingenuity as peoples and their governments, bankers, lawyers and technicians have found ways to make money respond to the challenges of new times. There is no road back from a society in which money is a key instrument of activity; that is not an available choice.

That is not to say that human societies do not have choices in the matter of money and its control. The reunification of Germany is an example of the will to make money subserve a greater political purpose and vision by allowing poorer citizens of the former East Germany a higher average rate in Deutschmarks for their previous currency than wealthier ones. The Jubilee 2000 campaign was in effect a demand that the world community find ways of making the rule of money something less than the final arbiter in human affairs, and the responses of politicians show that in principle, and to some degree in practice, that is possible. It is not impossible to take some steps to infiltrate even the volatile and uncontrollable workings of money with some element of mercy. That much choice we do have.

Again, the small but steadily growing movement for the reform of money is precisely the assertion that we do have some choices about the kind of money we use, the way it is regulated and who may create it. So too, small communities are able to create opportunities for poor people to save and borrow without allowing the wider rules of the market in money to determine interest rates. Further than that, local communities are able to evolve local exchange and trading systems (LETS) which permit the exchange of goods and services without recourse to money; at the simplest level many parents have experience of the points and tokens which baby-sitting circles use among themselves. We do have choices, and people are making them.

The lives of individuals also manifest the choices we have, and the choices we do not have. We have sought to show that money shapes us even as we use it: as we play by its rules so we learn them and tend to accept its rules in our lives. People may vary as to their natural greediness and generosity, their instinctive fear or generally carefree response to money; they may be more inclined to miserliness or profligacy. But whatever their response, money does things to them as they do things with money. Sometimes strong moral evaluations are attached to these varied responses to money, but from a Christian standpoint it is more important to notice for us all that there is no choice to opt out of the power of money to form us, only a choice to notice or not to notice. Including this chapter in a report on what it is, in Christian faith, to be human is an attempt to ensure that we do notice the choices we do and do not have in relation to the powerful medium of money.

In noticing that, however, we should also observe that individuals make choices with money that are potentially of enormous significance. Immediately this is said, there come to mind the religious communities of those who forswear the right to their own money. But there should also come to mind the fact that the marriage service makes no distinction between the unique bodily sharing that marriage represents ('With my body I honour you') and the unique sharing of possessions which it also enjoins ('All my worldly goods I share with you') – and we may observe in passing that as many marriages fail from the inability to negotiate the second as the first. The relationship of parents and children is (among many other things, naturally) a financial one, with patterns of responsibility and mutual support changing as children move into adulthood and parents into old age. Even though the use of money within our most intimate relationships can be fraught and often gives an appearance of altruism to what is actually quite self-serving, we do demonstrate there that we can exercise choices about the extent to which money will be allowed to dominate our lives.

The word 'choice' is in itself, however, of enormous significance precisely in considering the role of money in what it is to be human.

The lure of money is to a great extent the lure of the choices it offers: money in the bank represents choices that can be made now or in the future, and there is no doubt that for many who find themselves with money, having known only poverty, the experience of having choice is liberating. In this and many other ways the existence of money contributes to human well-being. But in the light of some of the negative effects of the way money has developed more recently, and which we have endeavoured to describe above, what are the real choices we face if we are to be human with money?

The choice between one slavery and another

We have described money as a good, but also one that has acquired a dominance in the lives of individuals and societies, and indeed on a global scale. The emergence of a human artefact such as money as something exercising a capacity to shape, and even to dominate, human living is something Christians regard as entirely familiar. It is the phenomenon of idolatry. A fundamentally ingenious, creative, productive invention becomes that to which there is no alternative, a force commanding fear and even a sort of obedience. Is there a risk that money might be God's rival for the right to shape human lives?

Let us examine some of the ingenious inventions in which money plays a key part, and discern its tendency to become more than a human creation. Insurance, for example, is in its origin a way in which human beings pool money in order to share a risk: we all pay a certain amount to insure against flooding, in order that the proportion who experience floods may not have to bear the whole burden of the disaster when it strikes. Similarly we can share the risk of untimely or accidental death, or of motor accidents. But what happens when this invention comes to be seen (and of course profitably promoted) as a universal protection against risk, as something which can be offered as protection against almost anything? Have we not then come to change insurance from being protection against shared risks, precisely measured by statistics, into something quite different, the fantasy of a risk-free life? From a prudent invention insurance is in danger of becoming something to be worn against danger.

Or what is happening when the game of placing small stakes on a chance outcome in a raffle, something that can be an amusing and enjoyable way of raising small amounts of money for a church or a charity, becomes through assiduous promotion a huge business venture on which, then, all sorts of society's requirements come to depend. Is not then a harmless piece of human playfulness emerging into a source of dependence as well as, in the case of some of the poorest people, offering a fantasy way out of poverty into riches, instead of what they actually require, the means of having enough and being freed of worry about the basics of life? Or what are we to say when the prudent instinct to make provision for the care of elderly persons is so played on that we are enticed into more and more elaborate means of saving money, as though money will comfort our later years?

We have already mentioned what happens to the benign institution of lending money when it is so promoted as to seem a necessary adjunct of life, and all our tomorrows are mortgaged and our freedom of manoeuvre sacrificed so that we can have today what otherwise might have had to wait until tomorrow?

As we go through these phenomena that illustrate the emergence of a human invention into the status of a controlling force in our lives (and many more examples could be given) we come face-to-face with the words of Christ, 'No one can serve two masters; for a slave will either hate the one and love the other, or be devoted to the one and despise the other. You cannot serve God and wealth (Mammon)' (Matthew 6.24). Here money is given the name of a divinity as we are warned against the idolatry of money.

The disciplining of money becomes, as we face our Lord's challenge, a primary responsibility if we are to prevent the shaping within us of what it is to be human from passing from God to Money. What might be the understandings of human being that would regain for us God's gentle rule in the governing of our lives? What might be the responses to the situation that we have described that might enable us, in the face of what has happened to the power of money, not to be conformed to this world, but transformed by the renewing of our mind (Romans 12.2)?

The gift beyond price

What being human before God with money means at the very least is the recognition that we are precisely 'human', of the ground, destined to be returned to it, earth to earth, ashes to ashes, dust to dust. This requires to be recognized in every aspect of living, not least those that constitute the central chapters of this report. But in relation to money it has a particularly poignant relevance. In common parlance it is money that is being referred to when it is said, 'You can't take it with you', or, in the more sombre and profoundly accurate biblical words spoken at funerals (no doubt in the presence of executors and inheritors), 'We brought nothing into this world, and it is certain we can carry nothing out' (cf. 1 Timothy 6.7). The contemplation of the sharp reality of dying relocates our confidence from the money we have amassed to the God who freely gives new life to the dead.

Christians have always been encouraged to show prudence and foresight, as part of their preparation for death, in disposing of their money (and other wealth) by means of a will, so as to relieve those who come after them of undue worry and anxiety. But the elaboration of techniques for tax-efficient maximizing of one's estate can go far beyond prudence and foresight, and express instead a very different motivation.

The practice of the Christian life affords ample opportunity for those activities and contemplations which have the capacity to dethrone money and place us before God, with our money, as human beings. The eucharistic meal with its echoes both of the free lunch for 5,000 described in the Gospels and the free gift of release and redemption places us squarely before the central Christian paradox of grace, that what is free most certainly is not cheap. That is, the experience of being fed without cost is to draw us into a self-offering without conditions. Before God are set the gifts of creation and the product of human labour at the same time as the assertion is made that we have these things only through God's goodness.

Likewise in the face of the generosity of God it is generosity we seek to practise (in the sense both of carrying it out and of constantly rehearsing it) through the generous giving of alms, and, it must be said, the joining in solidarity with the poor close at hand and far away in campaigning for justice though it may – and especially when it will – cost us. In the act of generosity we rehearse a dethroning of money as that on which we are tempted to rely for the protection and nourishment which come from God.

The regular practice of self-examination and penance is also an opportunity for facing what it is to be human with money before God. There is no shortage of evidence that increased affluence does not produce increased generosity: if money is a divinity it will co-opt into its ways those who have most of it. The generosity of the poor in comparison with the rich is well documented and is the common experience of churches and charities alike. The sharp, self-directed, questions, 'Am I better off than I used to be?', 'Am I being more generous?', 'Are some of the yardsticks of affluence (the car I drive, the frequency with which I eat out, and so on) showing me that I am in fact becoming less generous?', are rehearsals for a judgement which is God's alone and which will not exclude questions of our behaviour with money.

Money-discipleship has other aspects too. Avoiding unnecessary borrowing (Romans 13.8), restraining the fearful or covetous instincts which lead to spending more and more energy in the pursuit of money or savings, avoiding the flaunting of money to secure status or advantage (James 2.1-6) confronting the fear and apathy which lead to meanness (2 Corinthians 8 and 9), avoiding secretiveness and deception about our own earnings or possessions (Acts 5.1-10) – in these and many other ways we take a stand for the commitment to allow God, and not Money, to shape our lives.

However, no sketching in of our possible responses to the spiritual questions surrounding money is complete if we do not consider the way money is dealt with by the Church. The fact that money is asked for so much more often than it is discussed is itself the clue to one of the first matters requiring to be addressed. If it is the case that money has, for all its necessity and for all the creativity that has occurred in its development, nonetheless been endowed by us with the attributes of an idol, then it requires first, as idols do, to be named. For Christians to be able to speak about the fears, confusions and anxieties about money is the first step. But that may lead not just to a massive sense of relief for many people, but also to a new willingness to confront the demands of discipleship in this crucial area. Much of the Church's fundraising for itself bears the marks not of a counter-cultural resistance to the power of money but of a collusion with the fearfulness and ungenerous responses that are part of our culture's present stance towards money. The Church raising money seldom feels like a community overwhelmed by its joyful awareness of the riches it has received without price.

The practices described above, the practices of being human with money, are in reality central aspects of the practice of the presence of God. They recognize the point made strongly at the beginning of this chapter: being Christian about money is not a matter of not having any thoughts or desires you are aware of and ashamed of. Good thoughts will not arm us against the blandishments of money's pretensions if we do not address the behaviour which by its constant repetition schools us in the service of Mammon. Our giving, and our living humanly before God with money, is a matter of acting differently, of engaging with our money as with our bodies and minds in the worship of the Son of God who though he was rich for our sake became poor so that by his poverty many might be made rich.

Chapter 5
Sex

The Church has acquired a reputation for being negative about sex. So the first thing we wish to say (and it will be repeated throughout this chapter) is that sexual love between a man and a woman is a wonderful gift from God.

How the significance of that remark will be interpreted is, however, not at all certain. It has become almost impossible for citizens of a modern western democracy imaginatively to extract themselves from the acute sexualization of their culture. The combination and omnipresence of market capitalism and photography has resulted in a saturation of virtually all channels of communication by sexual imagery of an increasingly explicit kind. At the same time the invention of contraception has changed the way in which people can relate to their sexual desires, enabling them, if they so choose, to separate for the first time in human history sexual intimacy and reproduction.

This new environment has proved extraordinarily disturbing and challenging for the Christian Church. It is not that its traditions are too fragile or refined for the crudity of what is now on display. As we already make clear in Chapter 2, realism about sex is part of the biblical tradition, which is surprisingly explicit both about its goodness and delights and about its power to mislead and to wreck; wise sex, unwise sex, disappointed sex are all spoken of. The difficulty is more profound. How are Christians to fashion their response to their own natures as sexual beings in this cultural context? It seems we are faced with a forced choice. If we do not make a conscious response, then powerful forces at work in society will make that response for us. Our desires, even our self-understanding will be shaped for us. But, on the other hand, if we do not make a distinctive response, if we refuse simply to be constructed as consumers of modern sexual culture, what resources can we deploy to cope with the new elements in our situation? A merely nostalgic or conservative reaction is out of the question.

In what follows in this chapter we shall attempt first to describe the changing patterns of sexual relations in the modern world, and the secular views of sex which are widely taught or assumed. Then we shall seek an authentic response to the new context by speaking of God's own engagement with the world as the model for the interpretation of sexuality. We will revisit the Bible for an understanding of sexual union, and seek to interpret its meaning in Christian life. Problems and failures in sexual relationships will be acknowledged. At the same time we shall attempt to set sexuality with a wider pattern of relationships. Finally we shall describe what we believe to be the Christian virtues appropriate to sexuality.

As will be obvious from this brief survey we have stood back somewhat from current debates about exactly what forms of sexual conduct are permissible for Christians, and we comment only briefly on the currently controversial topic of homosexuality. There are two reasons for this.

First, this is a report about the Christian view of human nature, and each of the topics considered in this report has been selected because of its importance in that context. Sexuality is an aspect of human life in which the tensions between redeemed and unredeemed life are raised sharply. Also, sexual desire often reveals people's personality and character with disconcerting clarity; it is a place where 'the secrets of all our hearts are disclosed'. We are considering sexuality here because of the contribution it makes to a better Christian understanding of human nature.

Another reason for standing back from debates about sexual conduct is because we are convinced that those debates need to be based on a richer understanding of Christian wisdom about sexuality. Too often, Christians begin discussing the rights and wrongs of particular aspects of sexual conduct before they have adequately considered what the Scriptures have to teach us about the place of human sexuality with the purposes of God. That tradition affirms sexuality, but it also teaches us about how to judge it wisely, and how to work for its transformation. We hope here to provide resources of Christian wisdom that will enable debates about sexual ethics to proceed more fruitfully.

Changing patterns of sexual relations

In this section of the chapter, we will describe some of the changes which have occurred in the Christian approach to sexuality over the last 2,000 years, and also some of the changes in sexual practice that have taken place in British society over the last century or so. Our task here is descriptive, to provide factual background to contemporary Christian reflection on sexuality. We are not drawing any prescriptive conclusions from the changes that are described. Current patterns of sexual practices cannot be allowed to determine Christian teaching. However, their implications should be considered seriously in reformulating Christian wisdom about sexuality in present circumstances.

People are increasingly saying that sexuality can be seen in a variety of ways, and that there is nothing fixed or inevitable about the approach of the past. As Anthony Giddens comments in *The Transformation of Intimacy*, sexuality is now regarded by many as malleable, capable of taking on a variety of forms. Many now approach patterns of sexuality 'creatively', rather than regarding them as a given. Christians need to discern what are the anchor points of their tradition, and what can be rethought in changing circumstances.

In fact, there has been considerable diversity in what Christians have meant by marriage, and how marriages have been formed. For example, there have been changes in how marriage has been recognized in civil society, and in how the Church has been involved in that recognition. There has also been no consistency about whether the blessing of the Church has been sought for a marriage in a formal liturgical ceremony and whether such a ceremony has been seen as essential or optional, though within the Anglican tradition *The Book of Common Prayer* has given remarkable continuity to how marriages have been solemnized in church. The criteria for determining whether or not a marriage has been established have also varied, with some emphasizing pre-nuptial consent, others emphasizing sexual consummation, and yet others focusing on a public ceremony.

Over the centuries, there has been a gradual development of the relationship aspect of marriage in Christian thinking. Though that seems to us an essential feature of the Christian view, we acknowledge that little basis for this can be found in the writings of Christians in the first millennium. Hugh of St Victor, in the twelfth century, was path-breaking in placing emphasis on marriage as a 'conjugal community'. The reformers of the sixteenth century went further in developing a broader understanding of marriage as a loving relationship, reflecting the love of God for humanity. This is reflected in the threefold view of the purpose of marriage set out in *The Book of Common Prayer*, as for procreation, as a 'remedy against sin', and for 'mutual society, help and comfort'. Such views have long been important in the Anglican tradition. Jeremy Taylor in *Holy Living* (1650) was one of the first to expand on how physical pleasure relates to the broader functions of sexual union, not only 'a desire of children, or to avoid fornication' but also 'to lighten and ease the cares and sadnesses of household affairs, or to endear each other'. What was explicit in Jeremy Taylor was arguably already implicit in Paul's language about mutuality and a reciprocal giving to 'the other' in sexual intimacy (1 Corinthians 7.3-6). Language about the duty to give what is due is not so much about 'duty' as to ensure that neither partner is deprived of a pleasurable intimacy on the basis of some spurious argument. This recognition of the mutuality of pleasure stands in striking contrast to superficially parallel arguments about duty in contemporary Cynic and Stoic philosophical writers. 1 Corinthians 7.3-6 might well be regarded as an early Christian breakthrough, even if it waited for some centuries for fuller explication.

Though many now consider that a marital relationship is the ideal for Christians and should be the norm, that has not always been so. In the early Christian centuries, celibacy was often seen as the best condition, and rather negative views about physical union can be found. Again, some male Christian writers in the early centuries sometimes took a negative view of women, seeing them chiefly as a source of sexual temptation. On both points, this represents a failure to uphold the Pauline tradition. St Paul takes a much more positive view of sexual union than his contemporaries, and it is now almost universally agreed that the remark in 1 Corinthians 7.1 that 'it is well for a man not to touch a woman' is a quotation of a slogan misused at Corinth, and not Paul's own view. He was also innovative in laying obligations on the husband as well as the wife, and thus held a more reciprocal view of marriage than many of his contemporaries.

For some time now, the majority of Christians have taken a much more positive view than some of the early Church Fathers of the embodied nature of human existence, and would repudiate negative views about women. Indeed, the historical inheritance of the Church on sexuality is very ambivalent, and there are strands in it that now seem profoundly mistaken. Some contemporary changes are very much to be welcomed, especially the growing liberation of female sexuality. Others, such as the pain caused by widespread adultery, are alarming.

Turning to recent changes in British society, there are major demographic shifts taking place at the present time which form an important part of the background against which contemporary Christian teaching about sexuality must be considered, though they cannot determine Christian teaching. In the immediate post-war period, young people were deemed adults when they left full-time education and 'settled down'. The man entered the labour market and the woman began her household duties. But now, at the turn of the millennium, young people are likely to prolong their education and adolescence for up to a decade, during which time their financial position is precarious, and they continue to question authority. Not all members of this generation are likely to delay sexual activity until they get married, or to confine pre-marital sexual relations to just one partner. The widespread availability of contraceptives is both a cause and a consequence of this changed pattern of sexual activity. The spread of HIV/AIDS has to a degree also changed sexual practices, leading to much more restraint in some sections of society.

Marriage is also changing in character, partly due to increased life expectancy. In the middle of the twentieth century a fundamentally new pattern emerged of relatively early marriages which often lasted fifty years or more. This pattern came to replace the serial monogamy of previous generations, brought about by the death of either partner early in life, often by the woman in childbirth. As long life has become the norm, prolonged marriage to one partner has come under increasing strain. In the 1960s, almost every western society reassessed its divorce laws, and there began to emerge the possibility of a succession of marriages, albeit to a single partner, two or more times sequentially. This is also part of the background against which Christian teaching should be reconsidered, though again it should not dictate what that teaching should be.

We are also conscious that sexuality will be approached in different ways by different people. In particular, the sexual experience of women and men will be different, if only for historical and cultural reasons. We are still extracting ourselves from the ramifications of a culture that assumed that men should obtain sexual satisfaction, and that women should give it. There are also indications that the sexuality of men more easily strays beyond the confines of committed relationships; for example men are more likely than women to be interested in pornography.

Historically, western attitudes to sexuality have oscillated between libertarianism and asceticism. In fact, both may have a common root in the failure to sustain a high view of sexuality that sees it as a gift of God. As Roger Scruton points out in *Sexual Desire*, the over-puritanical views about sexuality that have sometimes surfaced in the Christian tradition are based on the same limited view of sexuality as the recreational approach that Christians condemn. Indeed, the development of sexual permissiveness in our society can perhaps be seen as one of the long-term consequences of the failure of Christians to maintain a positive Christian view of sexuality as a gift of God in creation.

Secular views about sexuality

There is a wide range of views in secular writers about the nature, function and influence of sexuality, and Christians cannot avoid coming into dialogue with them. Secular views have often taken a low view of human sexuality. Though there may be some value for Christians in such critiques, they are often pushed further by their advocates than is warranted. They are often put forward as giving an exhaustive account of human sexuality. Three such views, the Freudian,

Darwinian and social constructionist views of sexuality, deserve comment here.

Freudian theory, for all its helpful insights, has tended to see sexuality as a matter of primitive instinct, and to portray much of human life as arising solely from those instincts. We accept the Freudian insight that sexuality can be ubiquitous, and influence human life in many ways that are not acknowledged. We also recognize that it is often where sexuality is least recognized that it does most harm. The Church needs always to be vigilant for the damage that unacknowledged and frustrated sexuality can do. However, Freudian insights into sexuality have sometimes been exaggerated to the point of saying that human life reflects nothing more than sexuality, and that sexuality is nothing more than a matter of primitive instincts. Major Christian thinkers have critically engaged with Freud's work. Hans Küng and Paul Ricoeur, for example, accept many of Freud's insights, but firmly reject his world-view, just as they reject any claim that Freud's account of the human self is comprehensive or balanced.

Society has become increasingly aware of the dangers of sexual repression, and rightly so. Sadly, the Church has sometimes appeared to endorse sexual repression. Christian views about the role of women as subservient and undemanding have been particularly damaging in this respect. In contrast, Freudian psychology has brought to our attention the damaging consequences of repression. It reflects a tendency to keep the body at a distance, rigorously controlled, rather than being open to it and making sense of it under God. In contrast, the Church should joyfully and openly declare that human sexuality can be a matter of grace.

More recently, evolutionary theorists have tended to see human sexuality in purely biological terms, as nothing more than a vehicle for, and consequence of, the pressures of natural selection that led to the evolution of humanity. The currently fashionable evolutionary approach to psychology traces the evolutionary origin of sexual preference and behaviour. We accept that looking at human sexuality in the light of its evolutionary development brings many helpful insights. For example, the physical aspects of desire that can be important in sexual attraction may well have an evolutionary origin, and be explicable in terms of the advantages they once had in terms of natural selection. However, we cannot accept that there is nothing more to sexuality than this. Patterns of sexual behaviour arise from a complex interaction between biological and cultural influences. Human beings have become more than the products of their evolutionary origins, and not everything about human life is explicable in evolutionary terms. To see sexuality in an evolutionary context is the beginning of enquiry into it, not the conclusion.

There is sometimes a tendency to see evolution as an alternative to the purposes of God. However, ever since Darwin's *Origin of Species*, many Christians have seen evolution as the way in which God has achieved his creative purposes. Though evolution builds on random mutations, it has led to an increasing capacity for processing of complex information, and to consciousness. The result has been creatures who are capable of receiving God's self-revelation and grace, and we believe that it was God's intention that such creatures should evolve. Human sexuality, which goes far beyond the capacity for procreation, is one aspect of those distinctive human qualities that can be used for the fulfilment of God's purposes.

Another contemporary view of human sexuality has been developed from social constructionism. At its simplest this states that the concept of sexuality itself, and all our concepts about particular aspects of sexual life, are 'social constructions'. It also draws our attention to the fact that our present ways of constructing things are not the only possible ones, and that our concepts and categories have far-reaching consequences for human and social life. All that is self-evidently true, and it is helpful to be aware of it. However, the social constructionist approach is sometimes pushed further, and combined with the view that our concepts of sexuality do not refer to anything real. That leads to the view that human sexuality is nothing more than a social construct. The result is yet another critique of sexuality that tends to diminish it.

Radical social constructionism is also often allied with an unhelpful tendency to exaggerate the differences between the concepts of different societies, for example between the New Testament world and our own, and to minimize the continuities. We do need to remember, however, that the Scriptures were written in a very different age from our own. Some current topics, such as transsexualism, are not dealt with explicitly at all in the Scriptures. Other practices took different forms then from now. For example, divorce was generally undertaken unilaterally by the man, but had much more serious social and financial consequences for the woman. It is necessary to consider carefully how far these differences between scriptural times and our own affect the interpretation of the biblical message.

God's engagement with the world as context and model

The biblical story of God's relationship with the world provides us with the broad context for understanding the Bible's more specific teaching on human sexuality. The Bible is the story of God's engagement with the world, which is portrayed as a genuinely two-way relationship of love. The seventeenth-century Anglican poet Henry Vaughan depicted it as God's 'conference' with humans, by which he meant the kind of intimate interchange and companionship that good human relationships involve.

God desires and accepts love as well as giving it. God chooses not to be self-contained, but deeply involved with the others God has made to be his partners in the world. God is pained by rejection and abuses of his love, and God's love impels him to overcoming obstacles and damage to the relationship of love God intends to have with human beings. The biblical term 'covenant' expresses the wholehearted commitment, with mutual obligations, that God gladly and graciously makes to God's human creatures.

God's engagement with the world is both the context and the model for human relationships of mutual engagement. It is always God who initiates God's covenant with humans. Even though, as we have noted, there is reciprocity between the parties to these covenants, they are not relationships between equals. The analogy between God's covenant with us and the marriage covenant has sometimes been misunderstood as justifying inequality between marriage partners, but that is to press the analogy too far. The marriage covenant resembles the divine–human covenant, not in subordination, but in mutual love and commitment.

God created human beings, male and female, for relationship both with himself and with one another. Human beings are called to be both faithful to God and faithful to one another; human infidelity raises questions about fidelity to God. The Bible employs many images of human relationship to depict God's relationship to God's people: parenthood, friendship, political authority, and so on. But among these is the covenant of sexual union in marriage, which the prophets, especially Hosea, and, in the New Testament, Ephesians and Revelation take as an image of God's intimacy with his people. It is used to express the passionate delight in each other and the passionate commitment to each other that God and God's people can experience. There is a dark side: the disappointment and pain, even jealousy and anger of God's wounded love for his unfaithful bride, but there is also the promise of fulfilment and flourishing that the healing of a broken relationship will bring. As human love can thus become an image of God's love, so it is called to reflect God's love in relationships of human sexual union and mutual engagement.

God's engagement with humanity reaches its deepest point in incarnation, and God's healing of his broken relationship with humanity takes place in Jesus' passionate and painful engagement with his fellow-humans. The loving engagement between the divine persons that constitutes God's own trinitarian life in eternity takes incarnational form in Jesus' relationship with his Father, and in this way the inner divine love between the Father and the Son opens to include and to reconcile human relationships. Jesus' outgoing love crosses all the boundaries of social and religious exclusion, and it also calls for an answering response. He wants those he loves to take him to their hearts, as so many in the Gospels do: the woman with the ointment, Mary Magdalene responding to being called by her name, and the beloved disciple, all respond in this way. The kingdom of God as Jesus depicts it is the sphere in which people engage wholeheartedly with God and with others, both in selfless concern and in trusting intimacy. Not that the kingdom of God is a romantic idyll. Those who seek the joy of engagement will also experience the cost that Jesus warned us to count.

All this is the context in which we can understand human sexuality. Sexual engagement is mutually involving. It entails give-and-take, desire and delight, loss of control and self-surrender, the assumption of responsibility for each other. The degree of engagement appears in the fact that lovers see themselves through each other's eyes. A lover's desire is stimulated not only by love for the beloved but also by the beloved's desire for the lover. The self-revelation and self-surrender of sexual engagement is particularly risky, since both body and soul are uncovered, with the greater possibilities of humiliation and rejection this entails. Sexual union can be not only joyful and fulfilling, but also painful and disappointing. At worst it becomes a place of cruelty and perversion, mutual torment or ruthless exploitation. Both the promise and the failure of human life are intensively apparent in what we do with our sexuality, and what it does with us.

In the promise and the failure of sexual engagement we recognize the human condition in its need of salvation. There is both the glimpse of paradise and the awareness of expulsion into the wilderness of this world. Sexuality is one place, an especially revealing one, where the biblical story of God's engagement with human sinners works itself out.

The biblical meaning of sexual union

From sketching the wider context we turn to the Bible's specific treatment of sexuality as an aspect of our created being. The Bible does not treat sex as something whose meaning in human life is self-evident, or to be constructed by humans as they wish, but as something that is given its meaning and significance by the God who created us and is redeeming us. This expressed intention of the Creator must surely take priority in all Christian thinking about sexuality. Too many people think of the Bible's role merely as laying down rules for sexual conduct, but meaning is prior to rules. The Bible's guidelines for sexual practice make sense because they presuppose the meaning and purpose that God has given to human sexual union. Not surprisingly, we find this meaning primarily in the Genesis stories of creation and Fall (Genesis 1.27-28; 2.18-24; 3.16, 20; 4.1), which are normative for the biblical view. Later biblical passages on the theme, including those in the New Testament, constantly refer back to these passages, especially to the key passage in Genesis 2.23-24:

> Then the man said, 'This at last is bone of my bones and flesh of my flesh; this one shall be called Woman [Hebrew *ishshah*], for out of Man [*ish*] this one was taken.' Therefore a man leaves his father and his mother and clings to his wife, and they become one flesh.

Both the story of the woman's creation from the man's rib (verses 21-22) and the punning play on the Hebrew words for man and woman are ways of imaging the special character of sameness and difference that relates and distinguishes the sexes. The language in which these verses describe the sexual union ('bone of my bones and flesh of my flesh', 'one flesh') is covenantal. Similar language is used elsewhere of blood relationships, not just as biological connections but as involving commitments and obligations. The sense is that sexual union creates a covenantal bond, binding in the way that parent–child relationships are, and one which takes precedence even over the parent–child relationship of each partner to their parents. It is a whole-person relationship of love and loyalty involving body and self. 'One flesh' suggests both the physical act that unites the couple and the personal bond that is, we now see, the God-given meaning of that physical act. Hence this text becomes, in Scripture, the touchstone by which sexual practices are tested and found inadequate or opposed to the God-given meaning of sexual union.

Genesis 2 tells a story about the creation of humanity by narrating the creation first of man and then of woman. This has often been taken to imply a kind of hierarchical precedence of the man over the woman, but the text need not be read in that way. The temporal sequence is the way the story portrays the differentiation and mutuality of the sexes, not the subordination of one to the other. In the Song of Songs, the Bible's lyrical expression of the paradisal potential of sexuality, the lovers are equal in their mutual belonging to each other (see 2.16; 6.3). Neither in Genesis nor in the Song do the patriarchal and proprietorial constructions of marriage, as actually practised (and also critiqued) in Israel, appear: domination and subordination do not belong to the biblical meaning of sexual union, and there is no endorsement of particular institutional forms. Equality in mutuality reappears strikingly in 1 Corinthians 7, where Paul writes with evident care to attribute the same rights and duties to each sex. That the Bible does not endorse the patriarchal attitude that extra-marital sex is expected of men but forbidden to women can be seen, for example, in 1 Corinthians 6.16.

In Genesis 2 and the Song we see strong affirmations of the goodness of sexuality even apart from its procreative role. But, of course, procreation also belongs centrally to God's intention in creating us male and female, as Genesis 1.27-28 makes clear. Procreation is seen as a primary blessing of God on human life. Again, the key texts are quite free of patriarchal constructions (though there are some parts of the Old Testament that make patrilineal assumptions about inheritance, there is nothing of that in Genesis 2). Rather procreation is related to God's own giving of life, and the mother's role is not depreciated but highlighted. When Eve bears the first child, she says, 'I have produced a man with the help of the Lord' (Genesis 4.1).

The Genesis creation stories say nothing about other, non-sexual forms of human relationship (except parent–child). Elsewhere the Bible sets high value on sibling relationships, and there are two portraits of same-sex friendships (Naomi and Ruth, Jonathan and David) which are also, like blood relationships and marriage, depicted as covenantal bonds, even as (in these two remarkable cases) surpassing in quality the parent–child and the husband–wife relationships. Genesis 2 thus depicts a special but not the only form of intimate bond in human life.

In Jesus' teaching on divorce (Mark 10.2-12; Matthew 19.3-9) he refers back to the Genesis account and takes its understanding of the God-given meaning of sexual union extraordinarily seriously. Sexual union creates a covenantal bond as binding as close blood relationship, a bond established not only by the couple but by God. (It is a reflection of the nature of this covenant that it would be violated by divorce.) That covenantal relationship simply is the God-given meaning of the sexual act also appears strikingly in 1 Corinthians 6.16, where Paul applies Genesis 2.24 even to sex with a prostitute. Whatever the social context of the act and whatever the intentions of the partners, Paul assumes that sex has the meaning given it in Genesis.

But also characteristic of Jesus' teaching is his insistence that the demands of the kingdom of God can take precedence over all other human relationships, including marriage. This is true in some way for all disciples, but for some it requires celibacy (Matthew 19.10-12) following Jesus' own example of celibacy, a possibility the Old Testament had scarcely envisaged. Jesus puts it in a shocking and provocative way, that reveals, not a *general* depreciation of marriage, but the disturbingly overriding priority of devotion to God's kingdom. Paul's teaching is similar (1 Corinthians 7): marriage and celibacy are both good options, each right for those to whom God gives each gift. When the kingdom comes, sexual union will have no further role (Mark 12.25), but the covenantal love that it incarnates here and now will surely be broadened into an unimaginably surpassing form.

Sexual union in Christian life

Sex is thus a gift of God in creation. Inspired by this biblical view of sexual union, we believe that Christians should take an essentially positive view of the nature, purpose and potential of human sexuality. The secular world needs to know more clearly that the Church regards sexuality as essentially a joy and blessing. In Christ, we look with hope towards an abundantly rich and fulfilling human life, and that includes a joyful fulfilment of our sexual nature, and the physical pleasure it brings. The human flourishing that God promises us includes sexual flourishing that is both passionate and intimate. Of course, sexual life can give rise to many problems, and sexuality is often caught between the richness of God's promise and the painful reality of human weakness and perversion. Nevertheless, Christians should begin with a positive view of human sexuality, as of all other aspects of God's creation.

Sexuality can be fruitful in many different ways, as Christians have increasingly come to recognize. The fruitfulness of sexual union in procreation has always been emphasized as central to God's purposes for humanity. However, that is by no means their only potential blessing. *The Book of Common Prayer* also mentions the avoidance of fornication, and 'the mutual society, help and comfort that the one ought to have of the other'. Sexual union, at its best, holds together the physical and spiritual aspects of human sexuality that, in our society, can so easily fall apart. Sexuality can integrate 'ourselves, our souls and bodies'. Also, in sexual relationships people can learn the good news that they are desired by another. Sexuality fosters the kind of full and complete relationship that is often so much desired, and is so important in human life. Sexual desire is essentially a desire for another person, for relationship and intimacy. Though sexual relations bring physical pleasure, a search for sexual pleasure alone, outside the context of relationship, often fails to satisfy.

Another reason for taking a positive view of human sexuality is that Christians have often seen erotic love as integral to their relationship to God. Christians are encouraged to love God 'with all their hearts', and human sexuality can both reflect and enhance their love of God. Christians have sometimes seen the movement of the human soul towards God as a process in which the soul 'falls in love' with God, and the erotic love described in the Song of Songs can be seen as describing the love of the human soul for God. The soul is, in this sense, the 'bride' of Christ, an idea which is a development of what the Epistle to the Ephesians says about the love between Christ and the Church. Indeed, it may be one of the most important consequences of human erotic instincts that they make possible a heartfelt love of God. Human sexuality can bring a passion to people's love of God that it would not otherwise have.

Christians can properly see sexuality as a sacrament, in the broadest sense of the term. The 'outward and visible' aspect of sexual union can be a 'sign of inward and spiritual grace'. Our bodies can be part of our spirituality, not an obstacle to it, an insight that the women's movement has helped the Church to recover. Too often Christians have aspired to a purely 'spiritual' approach to life that regards their bodies as irrelevant, or even sees them as a hindrance to the Christian life. All aspects of the lives of Christians, including their sexual lives, can be a sacrament, in the broad sense, a sign of God. In saying this, we do not intend to over-spiritualize sexual passion and intimacy, but rather to say that our physical sexuality is part of the Christian life, part of God's gift to us, and falls within the orbit of his blessing.

The challenge to each person about their sexuality is how much are they prepared for it to signify? Are we prepared to approach our sexuality in a way that allows it to be a channel of God's grace and blessing? It can be helpful to apply terms such as 'vocation' to sexuality and to recognize in our sexuality something of God's calling. People may wish to ask how God is calling them to use their sexuality, how their sexuality can reflect his glory and extend his kingdom. Different people will give different answers to this question, which is as it should be, but even to ask the question can transform people's attitudes to their sexuality.

Like all God's gifts, the stewardship of sexuality can be wise or foolish. If we are to realize the God-given potential of sexuality, it needs to be shaped wisely. That can only really happen in the context of committed relationships, which is why such relationships are so important if sexuality is to flourish. The constancy and faithfulness of covenant relationships creates the climate of mutual trust in which the potential of sexuality as a source of human blessing can be most fully realized.

The wise shaping of sexuality requires both restraint about forms of sexuality that distract from, or subvert, its optimal flourishing, as well as a full-hearted commitment to a wholesome and enriching pattern of sexual life. Just as we need an educated conscience, so our sexual desire needs to be nurtured through a wholesome imagination that is looking towards the possibility of sexual integration and true sexual fulfilment.

Though the Christian approach to sexuality begins with the affirmation of sex as a gift of God, it does not stop there. As with all human conduct, sexuality is open to the light of wisdom of God's judgement about whether each person is using this precious gift wisely and according to God's purposes. God's judgement of how we use our sexuality calls for a parallel work of human discernment. Affirmation and judgement lead on to transformation. All of us are invited to join in the task of transforming our sexuality, as part of God's broader purpose of transforming the created order so that it fulfils God's purposes more fully and joyfully. Participating in such a transformation of our sexuality can help us to avoid being drawn down into failures of true engagement and relationship. As with other areas of human life, such transformation is often a lifelong task.

Sexuality should, finally, be seen in the long-term context of God's unfolding purposes. Human beings live in a time in which God's redemption of the world has begun, but not yet come to its final completion. We need to focus on ultimate values, but to remember that we live in penultimate times. In this between-time, sexuality is caught between the failures of the old order that is passing away, and the promise of the new order that God is bringing into being. Human sexuality is thus caught up in the drama of redemption. This calls for a double response. On the one hand, we should look and work for the continuing transformation and enhancement of human sexuality in accordance with God's purposes. On the other hand, we should not be unduly surprised or shocked by the more limited forms of sexuality that still often prevail, and show pastoral kindness to those who fail.

Problems and failures in sexual relationships

Where sex occurs outside the meaning and purpose God has given it in his created order, dangers arise for the participants. Some sexual disorders, such as paedophilia, are openly and widely condemned in society. However, it needs to be recognized that the sexual relationships of many of us share to some degree in the brokenness of the world. There can be a disturbing self-deception that regards sexual failure and disorder as something that belongs to other people, never to ourselves.

We live in a society in which there has been a growth in the commercial exploitation of sex, which is perhaps even more disturbing than the failed sexual relationships of particular individuals. A consumer approach to sexuality has developed that takes sexuality out if its proper context. Sex has become one of the main idols of our time that distracts people from God, diverts energy away from other concerns, and takes too great a priority over non-sexual fulfilments. The immediate availability of pornography in our society has created a polluted imagination that takes sexual attractiveness out of the context of relationships, and distorts the response to real sexual partners. Real people come to be seen, not for themselves, but for how closely they approximate to 'pin-ups'. Our society has developed such an inflated notion of sexual pleasure that the reality of sexual union can seem disappointing in relation to the fantasy.

In sexual relations, people exercise power over each other, give one another power, take power, lose power. This is part of what was meant by the feminist slogan 'the personal is the political'. Sexual abuse often takes place within contexts where there is already potential for a great disparity of power, such as schools, seminaries, churches and children's homes. In all these situations there should be a relationship of trust between more and less powerful agents, which should not be abused. The opportunity for abuse is increased where there is an ethos which serves to render domination invisible, and where there are no institutional checks and balances to temper it. But domination can occur even when it is not intended. Indeed, it occurs to some degree wherever one partner fails to take proper account of the other's desires, needs, fears and hopes.

In the casual sexual relations that are increasingly common in our society, there is the risk that the partners will feel no empathy or responsibility for one another. Even where there is mutual affection and respect, one partner may well attribute greater meaning to the sexual relationship than the other, in a way that results in that partner feeling hurt. Involving oneself in casual sexual encounters may also make it harder, or even impossible, to realize the full potential of sexual union, and the meaning which God intended it to have.

Some of the most painful failures of sexual engagement in our society occur when a relationship that was once the focus of a stable commitment and a source of blessing and fulfilment ceases to be so. This is especially difficult where one partner remains emotionally engaged in the relationship, but the other does not. An increasing number of people in our society have lived through difficult and painful divorces, to which there sometimes seems no realistic alternative. However, even divorce provides a context in which Christian virtues can be exercised, and out of which there can be a return to the joy that God promises.

Even if a marriage ends in separation, for it to break down through adultery is a very painful and destructive way for that to happen. An adulterous relationship can perhaps be concealed initially, but usually not for long, and there is always considerable pain when it eventually becomes known. People's desire for adulterous relationships often leads to the naive view that they will 'do no harm'. There is an urgent need in our society for greater realism about the consequences of adultery. Disordered forms of sexuality are often accompanied by an alarming degree of self-deception, in which people avoid seeing their motives and actions clearly, or understanding how their behaviour is affecting others.

On the other hand, it is too easy to draw the conclusion that sex within married relationships is always satisfactory. We should not imbue marriage with a halo of unquestioned sanctity. The reality of sexual abuse, even rape, within marriage has now been widely recognized. Marriage can also aid and abet disengagement in more subtle ways. The relative security of the marriage bond can make it easier for one partner to cease to pay proper attention to the another. Equally, married partners may cling to habitual ways of relating to one another, and so crush new growth and development in each other. Development and change on the part of one may be resented and frustrated by the other who feels 'left behind'. As the public commitment to marriage becomes rarer, and more a matter of choice, we are better able to see marriage for what it is: not only ordinary and everyday, but also heroic, demanding, perilous, and full of promise.

Given the almost inevitable failures of sexual relations, at some point each person will need to return to a proper focusing of their sexuality in the covenant relationship to which they have committed themselves. It is important to recognize the possibility of such restoration within God's purposes. There can be 'more joy in heaven', a more powerful experience of God's grace, in the renewal and restoration of a proper and healthy pattern of sexuality than in the rare sexual relationship that has known no problems. Though there will almost inevitably be disappointments in sexual relationships, they can be healed though forgiveness, which is an essential element in all human relationships. Through refocusing and forgiving, there can be a gradual process of learning and maturing in sexuality that will enable its potential gradually to be more fully realized.

The wider pattern of relationships

Stable sexual unions can also contribute to the ordering of society, and in turn reflect that order. That is as true today as it has ever been, despite the common insistence that sex is private. The self is not an 'island'. A committed relationship is not just two isolated individuals who meet in a sexual encounter. The boundary of their union is not coterminous with the boundaries of their two bodies, but has implications for others with whom they engage. Those who are joined by a sexual relationship relate to others by virtue of that relationship, and not just as individuals. Through their sexual union, each partner is also linked to the friends and family of the other, a linkage formalized in marriage by the creation of the category of 'in-laws'. By such means the sexual relationship connects not only with a future generation, but also with past and present generations.

The bearing and raising of children is the most important example of the broader implications of a sexual union, which extends to include the entire household. The commitment and security of marriage is clearly important for children whose identities are bound up with both parents and with their union. A stable, committed union, and the different contributions to parenting of husband and wife, provide the context for the social and emotional development of children. The breakdown of a sexual relationship means the end (or at least the disruption) not only of that relationship itself, but of the intricate web of other relationships woven around it. Thus, divorce often affects not just a married couple and their children, but grandparents, aunts and uncles, nephews and nieces, godparents and friends and the communities and institutions to which they belong. A whole new realignment of relationships has to be negotiated after the breakdown of a sexual relationship – often at great cost to all concerned.

One of the hazards of marriage and the family is that they can prevent engagement outside their narrow confines. Whilst few of the Church Fathers condemned marriage outright, many saw the way in which family life takes up peoples' time and energy as a good reason for avoiding it. Jesus' own teaching is also significantly subversive of family life. His question 'Who is my mother, and who are my brothers?' (Matthew 12.48) cannot be dismissed lightly. By proclaiming a kingdom made up of brothers and sisters of the one Father, Jesus rendered the institution of the family optional, rather than being obligatory, as it had been in much of Jewish society and its Scriptures. Jesus' message still challenges us when we use our families as an excuse for disengagement with other people and concerns. It reminds us that deep human relationships and engagement can be found in many places.

Sexuality will inevitably express itself differently in different people. Young and old will have different relationships to their sexuality, and there are particular ways in which it will be shaped and expressed in people who suffer from mental and physical handicaps. Though sexual union is an important form of human engagement, it is not essential to it. There is no record of Jesus himself being married or in a sexual relationship, and he does not teach that such relationships are necessary in the kingdom. The conclusion must be that sex is not necessary for the engagement that characterizes covenant relationships. The gospel challenges the assumption, prevalent in contemporary society, that it is only in sexual relationships that we can know real joy, real engagement, real intimacy. In a desire to dignify marriage and the family, the contemporary Church has often made it seem as though these are uniquely holy forms of Christian living, that they are *the* sacrament of human love.

Such a view represents a remarkable reversal of much of the Christian tradition, which has valued celibacy highly, not least because it makes possible forms of engagement which sexual relationship precludes or diminishes. Whilst there may have been good reasons for the large-scale abandonment of the ideals of monasticism and celibacy in the West in modern times, the effect has been to close down options for human living. The ideal of celibacy makes forms of living possible which are otherwise not easily provided, and opened up a space for forms of human flourishing which did not involve marriage or sexual relationship. Current evidence that growing numbers of people are choosing to live single lives suggests that attitudes may be changing again, and there is much in the Christian tradition which would affirm and celebrate that contemporary pattern. Now, as before, such choices are often made because people wish to dedicate themselves wholeheartedly to some other 'commitment', perhaps responding to a definite vocation from God to be single for the sake of the kingdom.

Human engagement takes place at different levels. At their best, even the most casual encounters can involve a certain amount of engagement, and we can be open to others – and to being changed by them – in even the briefest and most mundane encounters. Many people have lifelong friendships which involve the deepest intimacy and trust. They often involve an unspoken commitment to one another: true friends know they will always be there for one another and have a loyalty that lasts through life's ups and downs. For example, in some parts of the north of England men who are bound to one another by ties of comradeship and friendship call each other 'marrers', for their relationship can be as close as that of a married couple. Lifelong commitments do not always need vows, and to confine engagement to marriage and sexual relationship forecloses the possibilities of the godly society to which we are all called.

However, it would be entirely inappropriate to seek the deepest form of engagement with everyone we meet. Such engagement is in any case not a right but a blessing, and depends upon the freedom of another. The grace of which the gospel speaks is the promise that we can all know engagement with God; it is not always possible to experience such a depth of connection with another human being. Some people make a conscious choice not to seek such engagement; some are so damaged by previous experiences and abuses that it may be very difficult to achieve; some of us simply do not meet the right person.

Homosexuality

The statement, *Issues in Human Sexuality* (1991), called for further discussion of the subject of homosexuality. We believe that the Church's thinking about homosexuality needs to be placed in the context of the kind of broad Christian approach to human sexuality that we have set out here. In this brief section, we will first indicate some of the reasons why misunderstandings on this subject develop, and then indicate how what we have said about sexuality in general could be applied in different ways to the subject of homosexuality. Our purpose here is not to argue for a particular view, but to promote constructive discussion.

One major factor, which we have already discussed in general terms, concerns social constructionism. Radical social constructionists often maintain that the phenomenon of homosexuality as we know it did not exist until the term was coined in 1869, and that biblical material is therefore not relevant to modern homosexuality. The practice of homosexuality in Jesus' time was largely confined to the pagan rather than the Jewish world, and most often took the form either of prostitution or of time-limited relationships between males of different ages that were seen as part of the initiation into manhood. Biblical interpretation needs to trace both the continuities and discontinuities between the biblical world and our own, and care and responsibility are necessary in exploring the contemporary relevance of biblical material on homosexuality. We can neither presuppose its irrelevance to the modern phenomenon, nor simply assume an exact one-to-one match, without careful enquiry.

Different attitudes to boundaries can be discerned in the Bible. The view of sacred boundaries in Leviticus and some of the Epistles is sometimes contrasted with the outlook of the Deuteronomic tradition and the teaching of Jesus, which tends to abolish boundaries. Some might see Jesus' tendency to challenge boundaries, between for example Jew and Samaritan, as applying also to the distinction those who follow sexual conventions and those who do not. Sexual 'outsiders' are arguably only such because social conventions have put them there. However, not all boundaries are abolished by Jesus. Boundaries are essential if order is to be brought out of chaos. The question is not whether boundaries should be maintained, but which boundaries are necessary and which are merely human conventions.

Modern discussion often makes a clear distinction between homosexual orientation and homosexual genital acts, and assumes that references in the Bible are to the latter only. However, there are infinite degrees of variation and shading between the two, as there are also on the question of exactly what counts as adultery. In both cases, difficult boundary questions between disposition and action arise, and care is needed to discern the scope of what is being referred to. On sexual matters, the Bible does not yield the easy distinction between sexual disposition and act that modern discussion often assumes.

Reflecting on the implications of this chapter for the subject of homosexuality, some will think that the fundamental consideration is that, according to Genesis 2, sexual union belongs to a covenantal relationship between man and woman. They will also note our observation that in the Christian tradition the universal assumption until very recently has been that marriage is the only proper context in which sexual union should occur. To some, it will thus seem that we have rehearsed, albeit briefly, the fundamental reasons in Scripture and tradition why Christians should not engage in homosexual relations. Those who take that view will also probably wish to refer to other texts in Leviticus and St Paul, and to develop a broader argument about how same-sex relationships are 'unnatural', though those are not matters that we have considered here.

Others will accept that the covenantal relation between man and woman in Genesis 2 sets the paradigm for all sexual relations, but see no reason why that paradigm should not be extended to same-sex relationships. Noting what we have said about how complex and diverse the Christian tradition has been on many aspects of human sexuality, and that not all aspects of that tradition are now upheld (such as Christian attitudes to women), they might conclude that what the tradition has said until very recently about same-sex relationships is not definitive for all time. They might also note the broad view we have taken of the ways in which a sexual union can serve the purposes of God in ways that go beyond procreation; many of those godly purposes could be served by a covenantal relationship between people of the same sex.

Nevertheless, two New Testament passages are frequently cited as expressing disapproval of active same-sex physical intimacy. Romans 1.27 may well be part of a frequently used Jewish critique of Gentile behaviour, most familiar in Jewish synagogue sermons, and borrowed by Paul for a larger argument about respective Jewish and Gentile standing before God. In the light of this Jewish homiletical context, some insist that the allusion to a particular form of sexual behaviour in this verse should not be understood as explicitly expressing Christian disapproval of this specific behaviour, but as part of the stage setting for Paul's larger argument about Jewish and Gentile standing before God. On the other hand others insist that it remains part of a detailed ethical critique, which Paul himself appears to endorse. This issue is still under debate.

The second New Testament passage is 1 Corinthians 6.9-10. The significance of this second passage is also contested. One problem is how precisely we translate the Greek. Some argue that it refers to sexual exploitation rather than to same-sex intimacy as such. Another contested issue is that of context and form or function. Traditional interpreters insist that it is part of a Christian contrast between two distinct lifestyles, often formulated as part of an early Christian catechism, or instruction for baptism, about the distinctive nature of Christian conduct. Others, by contrast, see it as part of a catalogue of vices such as occur in several contemporary Graeco-Roman writers to formulate general ethical attitudes, and here borrowed by Paul for general rhetorical purposes. On this basis some argue that the specific ethical attitudes and actions receive less explicit emphasis than the general 'list'. This, too, remains still under debate.

In a different direction, some have appealed to the Council of Jerusalem in Acts 15 as offering grounds for a new approach, namely that of 'Spirit-endorsement', to issues of same-sex behaviour. They argue that it offers a counterpart to Peter's vision in Acts of a new order based on an experience of the Spirit's 'unlikely' blessing upon Gentiles or outsiders, and paralleled by later neo-Pentecostal phenomena such as the Azusa Street 'renewal' and the Toronto 'blessing'. Luke Johnson and Marilyn Adams argue that in each case 'taboos' and traditions are set aside. The Spirit speaks a fresh word. Other writers, however, including most robustly Christopher Seitz, insist that Acts 15 re-enforces an outreach long anticipated and prophesied. It is not 'new', in the sense of overturning taboos or traditions as such. Seitz stresses continuity, not discontinuity. This is a relatively new debate, and it is still in progress.

Whichever view we take of these three passages, the passages themselves cannot be ignored. What is important is that they are responsibly and honestly assessed, and their relevance to the modern world weighed in ways that attempt to escape self-interest and prejudice, in openness to truth.

There are various views of these matters, including the view that same-sex unions are not the ideal form of sexual union, but one that may be acceptable in certain circumstances as a concession to human weakness. On this view, same-sex unions would be seen, not as inadequate in terms of love and commitment, but just not the ideal form of sexual union. Such complex issues require very careful assessment in the light of Scripture, tradition and reason, and will be explored at greater length in a forthcoming guide to the debate to be published under the authority of the House of Bishops.

Sexual virtue

Sexuality is an arena of human life that calls for the full panoply of Christian virtues, and gives ample opportunity for their expression. Sexuality, because it involves our physical as well as our personal nature, is a place where people can work under God towards the transformation of the whole of creation, including their natural being. In cultivating sexual virtues, Christians are not eschewing the created order, but working to enhance and transform it.

Sexual union calls, above all, for that deep love that reaches out to the other person, respects their separate existence, tries to understand them accurately, wants the best for them, and meets their needs. The heart of such love is what C. F. Andrews called 'the accurate estimate and supply of someone else's need'. Such love, which provides the proper context for sexuality, is caring and considerate. It seeks to avoid becoming either smothering and over-controlling, or detached and hard-hearted. Such love requires great maturity. The nurturing of it is a long and difficult process that needs to recover from frequent failures and disappointments.

The emotional intensity with which a sexual union often begins can make it particularly difficult for the two partners to perceive each other accurately, and a special effort is needed to overcome emotionally based projections that distort what the other person is actually like. The romantic approach to relationships that is the norm in our society, for all its merits, creates particular problems in this respect. It is ultimately constraining and unhelpful for people to be in a union in which they are misperceived by their partner, albeit in a favourable way. Sexual unions need to hold together an enduring positive regard for one another, with a realistic awareness of what the other person is actually like.

People need to recognize that their partner may grow and develop in ways that were not foreseen at the start of the relationship, and to be prepared to give that their blessing and support. That is part of what is involved in wanting the best for the other person. Often, as the initial idealization of the partner fades, the relationship will need to be rebuilt on a different basis, in which there is an increasingly accurate mutual understanding of two autonomous people who, nevertheless, have given themselves to one another in a covenant relationship.

Love calls for faithfulness if it is to develop and flourish. Each partner needs both to trust the other, and to be trustworthy themselves. As the seventeenth-century poet Thomas Traherne put it, such love 'hath the marvellous property of feeling in another'. Reciprocal trust is a heart-warming blessing, and provides the conditions under which love can grow, and personal fulfilment can be discovered. It meets a deep human need to have a partner whose love is not hedged around with conditions, and who can be trusted to see the relationship through whatever difficulties arise. A strong mutual commitment can enable the relationship to survive times of difficulty that would otherwise destroy it.

Nurturing a loving relationship requires that both partners give each other time and attention. The pressures against making time for one another are considerable, given the demands of work and child-rearing. However, the prospects are generally bleak for a couple who have abandoned conversation, and whose friendship with one another has died. The means no longer exist to overcome problems, or for the relationship to adjust to changes in the personalities and interests of the two people concerned.

A strong and wholesome imagination is also crucial for a good sexual union that is beginning to realize its God-given potential. It takes imagination to reach out to the other person and to see things from their point of view as well as one's own. It also takes imagination to see beyond the inevitable human limitations of the partner, and to discern in them already something of what they are called to become as their nature is perfected in Christ. It takes imagination to see the physical glory and beauty of the partner and to celebrate that in sexual union. A sexual union thus provides the opportunity to cultivate the rich and truthful imagination that enables us to participate in Christ's work of redeeming both humanity and nature.

Most of the virtues required of a sexual union are virtues of relationship, rather than specifically sexual virtues. However, if the physical union of a couple is to work well, each partner needs to be willing to enter in the simple physical pleasure of it, and to be able to give and receive such pleasure. A sexual relationship calls for openness and a lack of pretence, and for a surrender of attempts to control the situation, or the partner. These sexual virtues echo themes that arise elsewhere in the Christian life, for example the surrender of control in a sexual union is analogous to the surrender to God in Christian discipleship.

The virtue of restraint is sometimes also called for if sexuality is to bring the full blessings that it can potentially bestow. The number of people with whom we interact in our complex society, and the widespread commercial exploitation of sex, means that sexual temptations will arise frequently. Some may be relatively harmless, there are many occasions when people need to refrain from responding to something that has aroused their sexual interest. Restraint is also needed within a sexual relationship, given the unequal power that often exists in relationships, and the way in which a sexual relationship can heighten vulnerability. To refrain from exploiting such vulnerability is not easy.

In every relationship there are times of difficulty, and that calls for particular virtues. It is important to have the clarity of discernment to recognize difficulties when they arise, and the hope, good-will and commitment to seek a resolution of them. Building a covenant relationship is a long process that calls for repeated recovery from failure and disappointment. Above all it calls for the capacity to forgive the pain and disappointment that often accompany relationships, and to be inspired by God's endless forgiveness of humanity to make a fresh start. In relationships, as elsewhere, Christians need to remember that they are not promised that they will be spared pain, but that God is able to bring lead them out of pain and difficulty towards blessing and joy.

Chapter 6
Time

Our times

How often do you think about time? Not, how often do you ask, 'What is the time?' or 'How much time do I have?' The question is, What is time? How is it to be used? Christian faith not only acknowledges that human experience is temporal; it also declares that time is God's gift to us, ingrained in the very fabric of the world he graciously creates. Faith also asserts that time has in some extraordinary way been taken up, reshaped and transformed in Jesus Christ. In this chapter we explore something of what this might mean, particularly in its implications for the way we live today.

Experiencing time

Human experience of time varies dramatically from person to person, and from culture to culture, and it is all too easy to assume that the experience of one person or community is 'normal'. For example, a person raised wholly in England who travels to some parts of West Africa will be struck by what seems to be a remarkably flexible attitude to punctuality, and will find social events timed with little or no reference to clocks and calendars (something explored to great effect in Chinua Achebe's novel *The Arrow of God*).

It is also the case that people's economic circumstances determine their experience of time. The way society is organized means that some people cause others to have different experiences of time. Those who are required to start and finish work at a particular time have less control over their time than those whose working arrangements are more flexible. Deadlines in work also exert their own pressure. The time of those without work may be subject to control by others: for example, by the need to 'sign on' and present oneself as available for work at a Job Centre; society is structured in such a way that it is reasonable to ask, 'Who keeps whom waiting?' For many the pressures created by having to live a life dictated by a diary are such that holidays and days off fail to provide adequate relief from the relentlessness of time.

It is clear that we can no more jump out of time than we can jump out of our own bodies. To be human is to be involved in time. To be human *now* is to be involved differently from being human at another time; to be involved in time *here* is different from being involved in time somewhere else; and to be involved in time *as ourselves* is different from being involved in it as somebody else.

In modern western culture, there are features which are common to the experience of time. Perhaps the most obvious is a sense of past, present and future. We are able to distinguish between a 'thick' present, in which our minds hold together the just-past and the just-to-come, and longer-term memory and anticipation, which have a crucial role to play in mediating our sense of past and future: so we remember the meal we had last night, we dread the driving test tomorrow.

We also have a sense of successiveness, which makes us aware of things cumulatively coming to be what they are; and we experience transience, as things pass away:

> Time, like an ever-rolling stream
> Bears all its sons away.

Related to this is our sense of cycles and rhythms: natural patterns of night and day, of the seasons of the year, as well as our own biological rhythms. Along with this goes our experience of what we might call 'narrative progression'. We celebrate our wedding anniversary every year, but we feel different each time round.

We know too that time can be either 'qualitative' or 'quantitative' – it can be measured in depth as well as length. As Rosalind observes in Shakespeare's *As You Like It* (Act III scene ii), time can also amble, trot, gallop or stand still, depending on what we are doing and what is happening to us. There is our sense of the right time. Comedians are praised for good 'timing'; badly timed remarks can cause huge damage; and an operation performed ten minutes late can mean the difference between life and death.

Not least, there is the sense of an open future: that however unchangeable some things may be, the future is more than the product of past and present, that we are not in thrall to a universe which simply unwinds inexorably like a gigantic piece of clockwork, but inhabit a world where there is 'room' for genuine becoming and novelty.

Time is not like any object in the physical world; it is not simply 'there' in the way this page is in front of you, amenable to description and analysis. Time is a dimension of everything we are and do, and even thinking about it is a temporal act. Reflection upon time by those who are themselves in and of time cannot extricate itself from the inevitable limitations imposed upon it by its own condition.

It is one of the main claims of Robert Banks's book *The Tyranny of Time* that a culture dedicated to the pursuit of leisure has, for many at least, produced just the opposite. According to one survey he cites, almost four out of every five people in societies like our own feel regularly rushed for time. Even if there are many who appear to be underpressurized – the unemployed, the disadvantaged, the prematurely retired – it is likely that 'The internal drives and external mechanisms that produce the time-scarce condition are the selfsame ones that produce its opposite' (p. 35). And the economic structure of the world demands that large numbers of people have their lives controlled by the material demands of just one small section of the world's population.

John Hull has written (in *Touching the Rock*) of the impact that losing his sight had on his sense of time:

> The measured pace, the calm concentration, the continual recollection of exactly how far one has come and how far is still to go, the pause at each marked spot to make sure that one is oriented, all this must be conducted at the same controlled pace. (p. 60)

Time could not be regarded as something 'out of which' things had to be wrenched:

> The simplicity, the careful planning, the long-term preparation, the deliberateness with which the blind person must live, all this means that he cannot take advantage of time by suddenly harvesting a whole lot of it. (p. 60)

In contrast to 'time-compression', he remarks that:

> When you have a lot of time, you experience time-inflation … You are no longer fighting against the clock but against the task. You no longer think of the time it takes. You only think of what you have to do. It cannot be done any faster. Time, against which you previously fought, becomes simply the stream of consciousness within which you act. (p. 61)

Significantly, for him, time was not an enemy to be controlled or defeated, nor something to be escaped, but as the medium in which things have their own, irreducible duration.

We might also note that no one is excluded from the disquieting fact of life that we are all dependent on other people to care for us for large parts of our time. Illness makes a difference to our experience of time. If we are unconscious, we know nothing about it – until we come round. But if we are obliged to lie in bed, or 'take things easy', we may either find this oppressive or be thankful for the relief that the experience provides from having to 'watch the clock'. We are dependent upon people to give us their time, sometimes in order to undertake the most basic tasks for us.

One way of gaining a Christian perspective on time is to take a look at western society and its recent history in the light of how it understands the relation between the human condition and the passage of time. First we shall look at the notion of progress. Then we shall turn to the question, Is it only the present that matters?

Progress

Since the eighteenth century the notion of progress has been especially influential on western consciousness of time. It suggests that there exists a potentially limitless, moral, intellectual, spiritual and material improvement in humanity and the world. Progress is thought to be built into the evolutionary process, and it also entails the mastery of the future through the application of scientific rationality, education and technological control. Such ideas were given greater impetus by the invention of mechanical clocks, which emerged in the fourteenth century, and which divided the hour into minutes and seconds. (In fact, the function of the first clocks was to assist monks to hold the day and night services at the correct hour.) The modern western sense of time has been hugely influenced by these developments, as time has been standardized into universal, global time, presided over by what many see as the key machine of the modern age, the clock.

However, it has become increasingly hard to sustain an understanding of progress, for it proved unable to take account of some of the basic realities of living in time. First, to be dominated by clock time is to assume that only those things that can be strictly timed and delimited are valuable; but we all know that many of the most fruitful things we do will not fit easily into calculable units of clock time.

Second, to view history as a single, unbroken line too easily encourages a smooth and homogenous view of human life that has no real place for interruption. Novelty is played down, and there is little room for acknowledging that we experience past and future as *qualitatively* (not just quantitatively) different.

Third, the culture which such a view of progress has promoted tends to ignore the fact of transience; it can nourish the illusion that humans are immortal, and that death can be postponed indefinitely.

Fourth, this marginalizing of transience helps to foster the illusion that our resources are unlimited. The myth of linear progress in time needs limitless resources, material, moral, spiritual and intellectual, along with an optimistic projection of growth. However, it fails to give weight to our moral and human limitations and the sheer interruptive force of evil.

Fifth, it is noteworthy that whatever the immense steps forward in our scientific understanding of time, we do not seem to be very much better at using it. Being pressured by time is a pervasive feature of contemporary life in the West; because our days are too full and move too fast, we never quite seem to catch up with ourselves.

Sixth, one of the ways in which our uneasiness with time is most clear is in various attempts to control time. Human beings have in every age attempted to defer or defy death; today, through medication, cosmetic surgery, healthy living, and so on, we have been given a range of new ways of holding at bay the inevitable drive towards decay and dying. But whether this has enabled us to live any more fruitfully in the meantime is debatable; 'We've added years to our life, not life to our years', someone has said (the saying is attributed to the American humorist, George Carlin). Another attempt to control time is seen in the frenetic attempt to grasp the future now; we have become addicted to urgency.

Another familiar type of time control is associated with the combination of clock time and industrialization. As we have noted, a very large part of western contemporary life, especially urban life, is strictly controlled by the hands of clocks – or the digits of timing devices. Where once the capacity of a person to work a piece of land in one day might be a standard time unit, now 'man hours/person hours' are calculated on the basis of universally applicable units of clock time. In other words, our sense of time has been removed not just from the natural environment but from any particular environment. What was once 'time in relation to this or that' or 'time for this or that' becomes simply 'time', that is, clock time. Linked to this has been the pressure to turn time into a commodity to be bought and sold. 'Time is money,' we are told, and 'industrial time' is a resource with both a use and an exchange value.

Is it only the present that matters?

One of the features of contemporary society would seem to be a dramatic 'speeding up' of time. Over the past two centuries, the pace of life has dramatically increased, and at the start of the twenty-first century this increase shows no sign of abating.

At first this process was aided by the shift from craft industries to centrally managed production line industries and the emergence of mass markets. Today we are witnessing moves to less centralized, more flexible systems of management, and a shift from production and consumption of goods to the production and consumption of services. With these changes has also come the explosive growth of information technology. The overall effect is one of ever-decreasing turnover times. What would have once taken a long time (for example, travelling to South America, or sending a message to New Zealand), now takes 'no time at all', courtesy of aeroplanes, email and satellites. Thus some have written of a 'compression' of time which leaves many profoundly disorientated.

The typical dominant attention of the postmodern ethos is to the present, the psychological 'thick' present and its prolongation, combined with a hesitancy about constructing long-term future plans. Many dreams of progress appear to have faltered, the very technological progress that has done so much to fuel them has played no small part in generating ecological disaster, a disintegrating social order, and the more fearful aspects of biotechnology. More than one writer spoke of 'millennial anxiety', a fear of the future that characterized British society in the last decade of the twentieth century.

The associated malaises concerning time have been highlighted by many commentators. We are faced with a division of our time into discrete types – family time, work time, leisure time, and so forth – and sometimes within each there are multiple times at work: those employed in financial markets, for example, deal simultaneously with many institutions and dealers around the world and around the clock. These different times criss-cross and pull against each other. Further problems arise when these interfere with our biological timing patterns of eating, sleep and exercise – and with the rhythms of others' lives – as when we're inundated with the constant interruption of telephone calls, emails or unexpected visitors.

It is said that we now interpret our lives less and less in terms of successiveness and narrative progression. Hence the evasion of a sense of duration in much rock video, the multiple dislocations and 'time-foldbacks' of postmodern films and novels (though it ought to be said that narrative is by no means dead – witness virtually any soap opera). We find it easier to cope with rapid change and an increasing rate of change amidst dreams of a better future, but with a weakened sense of long-term hope, with little in the way of a shared vision of the human good to which we might want to aspire, it is hard to know which changes to value and which to reject.

The strategies we use to come to terms with this disorientating complexity are many and varied, most involving a concentration on the immediate present, and many designed to stave off our fears of the future. Many try to squeeze as much as possible into a long working day. Others celebrate the ephemeral and elusive – immersing themselves in the pleasures, benefits and distractions of ever-shorter 'moments'.

In such a climate, our sense of the need for a continuing obligation to another person or persons can be easily eroded – it is much easier and safer to settle for short-term commitments and 'one-off' relationships. Enchanted with the transient, we 'sample' relationships, experiences, even religions, in the way in which a rock DJ 'samples' sounds for dancers from a multitude of sources and sets them over a rhythmic ground. Another strategy is to attempt some form of escape and evasion – to create a kind of simple 'extended present' into which we can retreat and avoid the manifold rush of our society. There is a growing and significant quantity of highly successful music which appears to offer just this: for example, New Age music, the 'New Simplicity' music of Tavener, Gorecki and Pärt, the 'chill out' music of the rave culture.

Whatever we conclude from this cursory glance at the ways we have come to shape our experience of time, it is clear at least that contemporary western society finds it a struggle to live in and with time in enriching and fruitful ways. Time is often treated as the enemy to be controlled, struggled with, perhaps even defeated, or else as something to be evaded or escaped. We seem to find it especially hard to live with the temporal grain of things, to be 'at home' with time.

The Christian Church has both profoundly affected and been affected by these developments. For example, though we might want to disentangle the dogma of progress from a Christian view of history, it is undeniable that the latter has played a significant part in the emergence of the former. Christians have also been prone to all the symptoms of the contemporary unease with time we have noted – a frantic busyness, a fear of novelty, a chronic impatience, a denial of death. Archbishop Rowan Williams has suggested that western society has lost the 'icons', the imaginative patterns, which once enabled it to hold a broad understanding of the human self.

The Church needs to ask whether there are major strands of wisdom within the Christian Scriptures and tradition – perhaps long suppressed or forgotten – that open up different and much more fruitful ways of living in and with time. It is this area that we shall explore in what follows.

God and the gift of time

Modernity has to a large extent been driven by a vision of time and history which places great stress on human agency and will. There is an assumption that time should be viewed as ours to arrange and order. Such a view stands in stark contrast with a Christian vision of time as primarily and decisively related to God the creator – the one who gives time to the world, and the one who (more than any other) gives shape to time.

To become a Christian is, among other things, to begin to live in time as given and shaped by God. More important, therefore, than asking questions such as 'What is time?' or even 'How should we use it?' is to ask 'Whose time is it?' The fundamental answer – more fundamental than 'ours' – is 'It is God's time.' The Ten Commandments contain an important marker of the significance of time in the plan of God for the world. The command, 'Remember the Sabbath day, and keep it holy …', presupposes that God takes time with the utmost seriousness. He works according to his own design, and he paces himself, as it were, according to what he wishes to achieve. So he knows when he has finished his work, and he takes his rest.

The New Testament makes the claim that everything God creates relates to the person of Jesus Christ. He is the foundation, the centre and the destination of all. The one 'in whom all things' were created (Colossians 1.16), is 'the firstborn of all creation … the beginning, the firstborn from the dead' (Colossians 1.15, 18), the one in whom God 'gathered up' all things (Ephesians 1.10-11), 'the first and the last, and the living one' (Revelation 1.17-18). If the phrase 'all things' includes time (as surely it must) and if in Christ 'all things' have found their fulfilment, then, presumably, in some sense, Christ is the meaning of time. Christ's time and history – his incarnate life, death and rising – are decisive for all time and history.

The first day of the week, 'the Lord's day', on which Jesus was raised from the dead, embraces both elements of the Jewish 'seventh day' and the celebration of the Resurrection over the forces of death. There is a strand of thinking in the Old Testament which suggests that the creation represented God's victory over the evil forces of chaos; for Christians, this victory is even sweeter, in that it represents also his victory over those same forces, now regarded as the cause of sin and suffering. So we celebrate God's rest from all the work he had done, both in creation and in redemption.

The reality of time

What kind of account of time unfolds from this perspective?

We are reminded, first of all, of the full reality of time as an intrinsic dimension of the world that God creates. In Jesus Christ we witness a fully human life, lived out in time. There is no hint that God evades, ignores, or tries to defeat time. He shares in it. In the eternal Son 'taking flesh', God confirms time as fully real, as a condition of the world he graciously makes.

In creating the world, God gives the world time, not as an afterthought, so to speak, but in and with the creation itself. Time is thus properly seen as inherent to the fabric of the universe. St Augustine insisted that God gave the world time as he created it, and this shows an interesting parallel to the view of the matter put forward by Stephen Hawking in *A Brief History of Time*. Hawking also emphasizes that the universe did not come into existence in time because time was not yet defined as a dimension, just as the direction of 'north' is not properly defined at the North Pole. This represents a big change from Newton's view that there is a kind of absolute time, emanating from God, within which the creation occurred. (This is an implication of what it means to say that the world is created 'out of nothing' – there is nothing 'before' creation other than God, not even time.) There is another sense in which God 'gives the world time' – in that, like a piece of drama, it takes time to be itself. As a recent piece of graffiti had it: 'Time is God's way of keeping things from happening all at once.' Temporal process and development are part of the being of the world.

Despite all this, there have been periods in history, including the history of the Church, when time's full reality has not been taken as seriously as it might. For example, for some the temporal world has been regarded as little more than a route to a (timeless) eternity, to be left behind or even escaped. The ancient Greek philosophical world was marked by a large degree of hesitation about the reality of time and of things and events in the temporal world. The world of time was regarded as the world where things were ceaselessly changing, a realm of decay, transience and death – in contrast to the world of eternity, which was a realm of changeless permanence. So the world of time was of value only in so far as it directed human attention away from itself to the (utterly other) world of eternity.

Such an outlook proved hard to combine with the Bible's uncompromising stress on God's direct engagement with this world – with all its change, decay and death – climaxing in Jesus Christ. It gave rise to some persistent and damaging views of salvation – for instance, the belief that Jesus arrives from a non-historical world to rescue souls trapped in history, liberating them for a future life which will bear little or no relation to life in time. (The 1995 Report of the Doctrine Commission, *The Mystery of Salvation*, especially Chapter 3, 'Saving History', drew a distinction between attempts on the part of the Church to 'rule' or to 'renounce' history, and opted for a third choice, that of 'redeeming' it.)

More recently, further problems have arisen from a tendency to swing to one or other of two extremes in thinking of time. On the one hand, it is possible to speak of an 'absolute' time, as if time could, as it were, stand on its own apart from things and events. The view is usually associated with Isaac Newton, for whom space and time form a vast receptacle which contains all that goes on in the universe, conditioning events and our knowledge of them, independent of all that it embraces, infinite and homogeneous. On the other hand are approaches which construe time largely or even wholly in terms of human projection. We may use past and future tenses, it is said, but this is to be seen as part of the way we organize our experience of the world; we cannot presume that there is some kind of time 'out there' which corresponds to our temporal language. One of the most oft-cited exponents of this tradition is the philosopher Immanuel Kant, who stresses that time and temporal relations pertain to the way in which the human mind organizes what it receives from the senses. The tradition comes in corporate forms as well: we have already noted how cultures and societies 'construct' their experience of time in vastly different ways – some would go on to question whether there is any point in assuming an 'absolute' or 'real' time which somehow underlies these differences.

Both extremes are more likely to hinder rather than help us in our questions about the understanding and use of time. Despite the enormous controversies surrounding time in the sciences and other disciplines, there seems no overwhelming reason to reject the common-sense, stubborn and persistent idea that our consciousness of time corresponds in some way to a dimension intrinsic to the way the world is. Time, that is, need not be thought of as an absolute container, nor merely as a mental or social construction, but more fruitfully as an inherent aspect of the way things and events in the world relate to each other. This accords with the views both of St Augustine and Stephen Hawking.

Some have seen Hawking's view that the universe did not come into existence at any fixed point in time as showing that there is no need for a creator God. Indeed, Carl Sagan says as much in the preface to *A Brief History of Time*. However, that is a misunderstanding. The important point for Christians is that the universe owes its existence to God. They have taken a variety of views about the relationship between God, the world and time. Christian belief does not stand or fall on whether the universe began at a fixed point in time.

It is in the area of scientific exploration that the Christian conviction that all things were created out of nothing – including time as one of creation's basic dimensions – is seen to be especially relevant, along with the conviction that the Creator has engaged with time (including human time) in Jesus Christ. We are invited to see time as given to the world, yet not in any sense 'prior' to the creation of things 'in' time, nor as independent of things and events. We are invited to see ourselves set in this temporal world – time-bound, time-laden and thus inevitably 'shaping' and 'constructing' time, yet not in such a way that we can pretend we have created time or that we are its sole or prime shapers.

The goodness of time

The other feature of time of which we are reminded by Christian believing is of *the fundamental goodness of time*. There is no hint in the Scriptures that time is a result of the Fall, that time is excluded from the verdict that the creation is 'very good' (Genesis 1.31). As part of creation it is subject to the effects of the Fall, but time is not opposed to the purposes of God; it was for the world's benefit and ours. Certainly the temporal world, and our humanity as time-bound, have been distorted and corrupted, but time is not something from which we need to be delivered – rather, our deliverance happens in and with time.

The implications of this are considerable. That time is built into the created world does not make this world inferior to eternity, only different. It is part of the basic goodness of the created world that it takes time to be what it is. Likewise with things within the world. If something takes two years rather than two weeks, that itself does not make it less good or valuable. 'Taking time' is part of the nature of things. Trees take years to grow into their full stature – we do not normally see this as something to bemoan. Children take time to develop and grow – we do not usually regard this as a failing.

A rediscovery of the essential goodness of time helps us approach transience in a different way. Transience is not a sign of evil or fallenness. Because a piece of music has a last note, does that make it futile? The fact that we are born and will die, does this make our lives futile? Without some hope of preservation and transformation, perhaps it does. But the fact that we are bound by birth and death does not in itself necessarily speak of futility, only finitude.

Most importantly, seeing time as something given and shaped by the God who is Father of Jesus Christ will serve to remind us that time is not God and neither are we. In other words, we are delivered from a twin idolatry – seeing time as something equal to God, and seeing ourselves as God-like figures shaping time.

To regard time as created gift means, first, that created time is just that: created and not divine. As with the other subjects of this report – money, sex and power – we are not to treat time as some kind of divinity. To allow ourselves to be dominated by our clocks or watches is perhaps the most obvious form of such an idolatrous view. We create mechanisms to achieve our desires in the world, and we then become prisoners of those very mechanisms, and the mechanisms in turn create further desires we seek to satisfy. This is the story of *The Sorcerer's Apprentice*; whatever form such idolatry takes, it can only be pernicious.

Second, to say that God is the one who gives time to the world, and the one who gives shape to time, prevents us from taking ourselves too seriously. As we have said, though we do indeed in a sense 'construct' time, this is only possible because we are born into a world with its God-given time and times, with its own providential ordering, and with its own patterns of day and night, biological rhythms, physical processes, and so forth.

The incarnate Christ and the shaping of time

What we have called God's 'shaping' of time climaxes in Jesus Christ. Time's positive relation to God, as a dimension of the created world, has been distorted in many ways, and in Christ these distortions are directly and decisively healed.

Crucial here is the affirmation that Jesus lives a fully human life conditioned by time. The Incarnation was not a tangential intrusion of the Creator's timeless presence into his world, an invasion from outside followed by Jesus' return to a timeless beyond. It was a life lived out among us and with us, in 'the time of our lives'.

The life of Christ is itself the climax of a larger history, that of Israel, God's covenant people, and the still larger history of humankind. There is a strong tradition, stretching back through the Greek theologian

Irenaeus to St Paul, which sees the whole course of Jesus' life as a re-enactment of the history of humanity. In the language of Irenaeus, Christ 'recapitulated' or summed up the human race in himself. He lives Adam's life, but radically reverses the orientation of fallen Adam. In Christ, oriented wholly to his Father, the sin of all humanity is undone and its destructive consequences borne on the cross. Sinful humanity died on the cross; true humanity, continuous with that sinful humanity but now purged by Jesus' death, rose on Easter morning.

In Christ, therefore, the judgement and restoration of humanity is worked out. This means that his time is uniquely the creaturely time that God intends, brought to its fulfilment. It also means that because in him God's purpose for the whole of creation have found their climax, in him all time is reclaimed as God's and re-centred on and redirected towards him. In some extraordinary way, all time has been redeemed and renewed in Christ. In his resurrection Jesus Christ affirms the value of the time of those whose time is otherwise undervalued.

The earthly life of Jesus is the embodiment of what living wisely in and with time is all about; it is God's gift to us of a life perfectly 'timed' by God. The temporal virtues – and below we speak of patience, alertness and hope in particular – are seen in their fullness in him. We witness a life not driven by a damaging obsession with time control, nor by an attempt to escape the conditions of time, but a life of steady trust and responsiveness – in the midst of our time-bound world – to the one he knows as *Abba*, Father, the one who gives time. Here the twin idolatries we spoke about – of time and of ourselves – are entirely absent: only God is worshipped.

However, there is much more to say than this. For Jesus deals with the disruptions which human error and guilt bring to the temporal character of our lives. Above all, at Golgotha, God submits to death, transience at its most menacing – death not simply as the end to life but (because of human sin) as that which threatens to rupture our relationship with God altogether, and threatens to destroy any sense of point or purpose in life. On Easter Day, in the raising of the crucified Jesus, we are confronted with an event which radically and decisively overcomes transience. The resurrection of Jesus from the dead is a dramatically new event, not just in the sense of being unprecedented, but in the sense that it never grows old, or passes away. It never falls back into an ever more distant remoteness, it does not run into dark forgetfulness or some vacuity of permanently lost events.

This astounding and never-old event is presented in the New Testament texts as an anticipation of the goal of creation, a kind of preview of what will be. The day for which Israel yearned, when the Jews would be liberated from their enemies, when God's justice and salvation would be made known and spread to the rest of the world, and when the dead would be raised – this day has taken place in Jesus Christ. So it is misleading to speak of the new heaven and the new earth – of which the resurrection of Jesus is a sign and pledge – as the scrapping of this temporal world. It is more akin to God bringing out the world in a new edition – renewed and transfigured, liberated from its bondage to decay, and enjoying a full and final participation in the eternity of God. The imagery of this in Scripture and tradition is that of pregnancy, of coming to birth, of looking forward and of joy.

Therefore, though it may strain our imagination to the limits to think about it, the ultimate goal does not entail the 'end of time' in the sense of the abolition of time, for time, as a real and inherently good (albeit fallen) dimension of the cosmos, will surely find its own kind of renewal. The 'end' will, so to speak, happen to the whole extent of history. And it would surely be inadequate to envisage this as a matter of God merely preserving time and history in his memory, or as the mere recovery of everything that has passed away in this life – as if in a complete videotape of the whole of history. For although the new creation will share in the eternity of God, and enjoy a new kind of time – a time without transience and loss – there will be novelty, not the kind of novelty which lessens or replaces the old (as in this life), but a novelty where there can be addition without subtraction, an ever-increasing abundance, indefinite expansion.

Music offers perhaps the closest model – when one note has another added to it to make a chord, the second does not lessen or displace the first, they enhance each other. There is mutual enrichment, expansion. There is newness without loss or diminution. Applied to human beings, this would mean that the whole of our lives – from birth to death – will be redeemed from transience, and from evil and suffering. But presumably our lives will also need to be completed and renewed, made new. It is hard to imagine this completion and renewal being possible without the possibility of newness in the new world.

However hard this may be to express in words – and our language inevitably breaks down – the matters at stake are crucial: does our humanity finally matter to God? Presuming the answer is 'Yes', does the fact that we are thoroughly temporal contribute to our identity? Again the answer must be 'Yes'. Our involvement with time, then, has in some manner to be 'carried through' to the new heaven and new earth with the rest of us.

Even so, this can all sound extremely remote. So it is here we must remember and highlight another clear strain of New Testament teaching. The Spirit is implementing now what will one day be known in all its fullness. This new world order is ours to taste and enjoy through the Spirit, as we share in the new, 'redeemed time' of Jesus Christ. The new creation is already being anticipated in provisional forms in this life, when the Spirit gives us back 'the time of our lives', human time healed and renewed in Christ.

The 1991 Report of the Doctrine Commission, *We Believe in the Holy Spirit*, drew attention to the fact that, in the New Testament, the gift of the Holy Spirit means that the end of the age had dawned, and that the future had to do with a sense of temporal immediacy.

> How the new and innovative is related to the future is seen more clearly in the realm of redemption. In the New Testament the experience of the Holy Spirit is an experience of release and freedom ... Human beings remain under the law as long as the determining principles of their lives emerge out of their own past decisions and actions, and out of past choices and values reflected in human cultures and societies ...

> Sonship, redemption and freedom all have future aspects, yet to be fulfilled. But because the Spirit has already been given as the first-fruits of a harvest to come, the future is guaranteed ... is anticipated, as it were, in advance.

The time of our lives – in worship

It is the claim of the Church that we participate in this 'shaping' of time through worship. All true worship of God takes place in Spirit and in truth, because God is Spirit. It therefore takes place inside the fellowship with God through Jesus Christ which God has already established, and it is inspired and raised by the Holy Spirit. In this way, the 'spare time' we devote to worship is not that at all: it is a participation in God's own time, a broadening, deepening, extending and transforming of ordinary time in an extraordinary way.

We can say more. As human beings we bring to worship the totality of our beings – 'ourselves, our souls and bodies'. To live and understand the time of one's life is not simply to do so on its own terms, but in relation to the wider drama of God's dealings with the world. Our lives are an integral part of a huge story which embraces all that is, including the non-human creation.

Several writers have turned their hand to reflect on the relationship between time and worship, and here we note three within the Anglican tradition: Richard Hooker, George Herbert and Lancelot Andrewes. In Volume 5 of his *Laws of Ecclesiastical Polity* Richard Hooker (*c*.1554–1600) shows an acute understanding of different ways in which time is redeemed by the life of God among us:

- We start with God's initiative in creating the unity between himself and humanity, through a journey of distance: 'God has deified our nature, though not by turning it to himself, yet by making it his own inseparable habitation.'

- Second, that unity is mutual: 'participation is that mutual hold which Christ hath of us and we of him'.

- Third, baptism begins this new life sacramentally, and the Eucharist continues it: 'the grace which we have by the holy Eucharist doth not begin but continue life'.

- And fourth, we need a scheme of sacred time in order to encompass the mighty works of God celebrated in the seasons: 'because time in itself can receive no alteration, the hallowing of festival days must consist in the shape or countenance which we put upon the affairs that are incident to those days'.

Each one of these stages is linked to the other and involves time. The reality of redemption affects human beings in ways that can be sensed and apprehended, since we are God's dwelling. These tangible ways have a coherence about them, starting at the font and moving to the altar. They are interpreted both through the narratives of the Scriptures, and through the memory of the community. The times and seasons make up the daily rhythms of morning and evening prayer; the weekly rhythms of Sunday, the first day of the week, the day of the new creation; as well as the yearly rhythms of the Easter and Christmas cycles, and the calendar of saints' days.

Time is also a critical dimension in the rites of passage and the sacraments of the Church. Rites of passage relate primarily to particular life experiences such as thanksgiving after birth, marriage, and death. In these time is measured both by the age of the person concerned and by the depth of the occasion, for example, for the relatives of someone who is dying. Such rites can therefore be very corporate occasions, at which, as in other great liturgies, people sometimes say that 'time stood still'. The two so-called 'dominical' sacraments of baptism and Holy Communion offer a different series of perspectives. Although in recent centuries baptism has been associated with birth, candidates can rightly come from any age, as both contemporary experience and ancient evidence demonstrate. The essential time factor about baptism is that it should only happen *once* in a person's life, and any further expressions of commitment, whether at confirmation, or at rights of reconciliation, are therefore derivative of baptism. The catechumenate, with its stress on enrolment and Christian formation, at its best builds up to the unique moment of baptism, characterized in the Easter Vigil liturgy, in which the candidate 'dies and rises' spiritually with Christ (Romans 6.3-11). It is the Eucharist's function, on the other hand, to be repeated frequently, as Christ's command in St Paul's account of the Last Supper indicates (1 Corinthians 11.25-26). To use the language of many of the writers of the seventeenth-century Anglican tradition, we enter sacramentally the covenant of grace at the font, and renew it at the Lord's Table. It is thus baptism's task to initiate, and Eucharist's task to renew. This is one of the reasons why liturgies of baptism and Eucharist are central to the Church's proclamation of the gospel, and why, located in time as they are, what they say and what they do matter a great deal.

A strong theme in the writings of George Herbert (1593–1633) is that of providence. Herbert wrote two poems on baptism in *The Temple*. In them he brings providence into focus in the context of time and worship, particularly in baptism.

> In you Redemption measures all my time,
> And spreads the plaister equall to the crime.
> You taught the Book of Life my name, that so
> What ever future sinnes should me miscall,
> Your first acquaintance might discredit all.

Herbert's 'plaister equall to the crime' is the lump of figs applied to the boil which confined King Hezekiah to his sick-bed (Isaiah 38.21). Baptism, which 'measures all my time', is a sign of new life, and forgiveness of sins, past, present and future. Herbert's second poem on baptism opens on a complementary note:

> Since, Lord, to thee
> A narrow way and little gate
> Is all the passage, on my infancie
> Thou didst lay hold, and antedate
> My faith in me.

The 'gate' is perhaps an echo of a prayer in the Baptism Service ('open the gate unto us that knock; that this infant may enjoy the everlasting benediction of thy heavenly washing'). It is the opportunity which God presents to the human race – and yet he knows us before we arrive there, and believes in us before we do. Herbert's grasp of the human predicament makes him a strikingly contemporary-sounding poet, especially when he writes about our lack of self-esteem in this way.

Lancelot Andrewes (1555–1626) was one of the great preachers of the early seventeenth century, and he had something to say about the relationship between eternity (God's time), history (our time) and human reception. Preaching on 1 Corinthians 5.7-8 (Authorized Version), 'Christ our passover is sacrificed for us', Andrewes refuses to countenance an internalized, individualistic approach to the Easter Eucharist. 'It is not mental thinking or verbal speaking: there must be somewhat done, to celebrate this memory.'

There is always a tendency to turn the symbols of religious practice into visual aids, reminders of what Jesus apparently did a long time ago. But the stuff of worship in time, whether it is the water of baptism, or the hand-laying at confirmation, marriage, ordination, or healing, or the carrying of the cross on Good Friday – all these, and much else besides, are neither thoughts nor words, but deeds in our time, vehicles of eternal redemption now. And that sense of the reality of past, present and future being brought together in our life in Christ, and in the eucharistic celebration, Andrewes sums up in his concluding words:

> There is a further matter yet behind: for as this feast looketh back, as a memorial of that, is already past and done for us; so doth it forward, and is to us a pledge of another, and a better yet to come, the feast of the marriage of the Lamb here, that is our passover: where, whosoever shall be a guest, the angels pronounce him happy and blessed for ever.

Certain implications follow from the insights of these three early Anglican theologians that worship is sharing through the Spirit in the life of Christ:

- First, we discover our identity by being caught up in the true story. To be a Christian is to live and understand one's life not solely in its own terms but in relation to the wider temporal drama of God's dealings with the world, including the non-human creation.
- Second, worship is the refusal of all idolatries; we discover the primary giver and shaper of time; we are delivered from the twin idolatries mentioned above – of treating time as God, and from trying to assume a god-like status with respect to time. It is not that other loyalties and powers are denied or demonized; rather, they are made relative to the sovereignty of God, who alone commands obedience – above, among other things, those very realities of human life which are addressed in this report: money, sex and power. This

is implicit in the ascription of praise at the end of the Lord's Prayer, 'For the kingdom, the power and the glory are yours ...'

• Finally, worship grants us a sense of the redeemed 'time' established in Jesus Christ, an experience of an interweaving of past, present and future which we shall eventually enjoy in fullness – a future, anticipated in the past, which transforms the present, involving the carrying forward of what is good (nothing valuable to God will be allowed to pass away), the forgiving of the past (a bad past is never the last word), and a sense of the 'ever-new' life of the new heaven and earth.

The main coordinates of living in 'redeemed time' are provided in the Church's pattern of worship in its yearly, weekly and daily rhythms, and this marks not only the passage of time, but also the stages of the Christian life. The yearly rhythm is provided by the Church's Year, and the weekly by the observance of Sunday and the daily by reading and praying the Offices.

The Year provides two perspectives on time, which is the structure through which the coordinates of word and sacrament are mediated: one perspective comprises the Seasons and the other comprises the Holy Days. Seasons provide an overall view, while Holy Days perform two functions: they mark and highlight the Seasons, and they punctuate them with celebrations of saints – and thus remind the Church that God's time is not always as ordered and as free-flowing as the calm patterning of the seasons might suggest. God can surprise.

The Christian Sunday, which replaces the Jewish Sabbath, provides the context for the celebration of the Resurrection 'on the first day of the week' in the Eucharist. It may be true that many people in our society are now unaware the Sunday is the first day of the week; and it may also be true that many Christians, including Christian clergy, have become accustomed to diaries which start the week with Monday. Yet for all the convenience of being able to look ahead and plan for the Lord's Day, we do well to recall that it is the Lord who starts the week.

All the main religions have some such weekly observance: for Muslims it is Friday, for Jews it is Saturday. The Christian Sunday now has a twofold role. One role of Sunday is to recall and celebrate the resurrection of Jesus from the dead. This celebration takes place primarily in the Eucharist; and, as we have noted, it is here that the time of this world is linked with God's eternity. The other role, in so far as Sunday recalls the Jewish Sabbath, is to remind humanity of the need for regular rest from work.

Christian people are called to take up their cross *daily* and follow Christ. The preoccupation of the Churches with rewriting their eucharistic liturgies over the past years has perhaps obscured the degree to which the praying of the daily Offices of Morning and Evening Prayer allowed and encouraged lay people to pray regularly without the assistance of a member of the clergy. If this tendency could be reversed, and all the people of God encouraged to pray regularly, the effects on the life of Church and nation could be considerable. The recital of psalms, the reading of Scripture, the singing of canticles and hymns and the saying of prayer is a gift and skill which the Church desperately needs to recover. It may be significant that in churches, especially Cathedral churches, where this happens, attendance at the Office is remarkably high.

Virtues and habits – 'keeping in time'

What follows by way of conclusion to this chapter is a brief series of practical reflections on how Christians might keep alive a sense of our involvement in God's new time. Much more could be said, and it is hoped that these reflections will stimulate others.

In a culture so concerned with the wise 'use' of time, it is important to work out wise patterns of life, outside the context of corporate worship as well as within it. The main strands of this chapter are drawn together by reference to 'temporal virtues', habits of life which are formed through living 'in time' with Christ in the Spirit. They are set out in pairs, to draw attention to their interrelated nature. Taken seriously, and lived out joyfully, they may challenge and subvert many of the cherished assumptions about time which govern our lives.

Patience and faithfulness

Patience arises from taking the reality and goodness of God's gift of time seriously and recognizing that some things are such that we simply have to wait for them. Certain art forms are well equipped to help us learn this kind of waiting, and music, the most time-conditioned of the arts, is one of them.

Music cannot be rushed; it schools us in the art of patience. Certainly, today's technology means that we can hop from excerpt to excerpt on a CD; but few would claim they hear a work in its integrity by doing this. We can sing or play a piece faster, but only to a very limited degree before it becomes unintelligible. Music asks for my patience, my trust. It does this without promising some identifiable 'thing' we can take away with us when the music is over, something which shows us that it was 'worth the wait', yet the waiting which music demands is usually experienced as anything but pointless or vain. Music can teach us a kind of patience which stretches and enlarges, deepens us in the very waiting.

Something of this kind of patience and waiting can, it would seem, be learned in the midst of tragedy and trauma, as the above reference to John Hull illustrated.

There is another kind of patience, especially hard to cultivate, namely patience in the midst of what seems to be pointless and destructive delay. The Christian life is by its nature lived in the midst of an often bewildering 'deferred gratification', a delay of the day when, in the words of Romans 8, nothing shall separate us from the love of God in Christ (Romans 8.35-39).

Human patience can be very closely linked to God's own forgiving patience. God's refusal to bring things quickly to a close does not indicate inertia or abandonment (nor compliance or indulgence) but is full of his longing that the world be saved (2 Peter 3.9). This bears on the kind of patient forgiveness we are to show to others: divine and human patience are brought together powerfully in the parable of the unforgiving servant (Matthew 18.21-35). Certainly, delay can at times be anything but enriching – the psalmist cries out of an experience of agonizing delay: 'How long?'; but patience is one of the marks of authentic love (1 Corinthians 13.4).

Faithfulness, which we may set alongside patience, lends time a quality by providing us with a point of focus for our waiting. During the passing of our time we are called to be faithful to God and to whatever it may be to which he has called us.

Faithfulness in worship can enable us to take time seriously, to note its rhythms and to give thanks for them, to recall us both to remember God's gracious acts in time and to look forward with joy to God's future, when all things will be 'gathered into one' in Christ.

Faithfulness in our behaviour and actions will mean that we use our time well. It may also invite us to take the time to consider seriously *how* we act, and the sacrament of reconciliation is one way of doing this. Ephesians 5.16 speaks of 'making the most of' (or 'redeeming') 'the time'. This is a way of being careful how we live, 'not as unwise people but as wise'.

Wise Christians will examine their actual behaviour and seek to orientate themselves towards good relationships. Ephesians 5 then develops the 'household codes', which show how interdependence within the home can demonstrate the life of the Christian household lived in the light of Christ's constant presence.

Forgiveness and gratitude

Forgiveness lies at the very heart of the Christian gospel. If we take seriously the example of Jesus, we see that it is not a special virtue called forth only by sin and sinners, but a fundamental disposition. Like love, forgiveness is the attitude with which we should approach every person we meet, intimate and stranger alike.

What forgiveness does is to transform time. Above all, it sets the present and the future free from captivity to the past. To approach people with forgiveness is to refuse to allow our memories, our accumulated impressions, our habituated responses, to determine how we relate to them. It is to start afresh each time. It is to approach someone as a *living* being and to allow them a present and a future which are not determined by their past.

To forgive, and to be forgiven, is to be allowed to escape. It is to be set free from a destructive past into the future of a God who makes all things new.

Gratitude is a way of looking back with pleasure at what has taken place in the past. To say 'thank you' is one of the primary courtesies that keeps our society flourishing – and gratitude, or thanksgiving, is the first idea in nearly all of St Paul's Letters. It has even been suggested that he bases his theology upon it. The Gospels also have frequent references to Jesus 'giving thanks'.

Gratitude for the past and for all that we see of God in the present will not be blind either to the sin for which we are responsible or the suffering which we bear; but it will acknowledge the forgiveness we have been granted and the lessons we have consequently learned about the faithfulness of God and about our own selves. It will also awaken us to the possibility of a future lived in hope.

When the Church gives thanks, it 'praises him for his glory': it expresses gratitude for who God is and for what he has done by creating the world and giving it time, in entering that time in the person of Jesus in order to bring about its ultimate salvation, and in being present by his Holy Spirit in every human moment. Christian people see these truths of the gospel both embedded in our past and present to our contemporary awareness of the world. We might therefore look for opportunities to see them and give thanks for them constantly.

Alertness and rest

The virtue of *alertness* takes seriously the call to be vigilant and seize the opportunities that God gives. It is not the same as frantic rush or tension. A certain urgency to seize the moment resonates through the teaching of Jesus, and is formulated in the Gospel summary of his message: 'The time is fulfilled, and the kingdom of God has come near; repent, and believe in the good news' (Mark 1.15). The fourth evangelist keeps his readers in temporal suspense with Jesus' repeated awareness that his 'hour' had not yet come (John 2.4; 7.6), until at last he recognizes its arrival (John 12.23), facing it with the anguish and acceptance (John 12.27) that the other Gospels portray in Jesus' prayers in Gethsemane. As a result of what God has done 'in the fullness of time' in Christ, New Testament writers recognize the time in which they live as *the* time of God-given opportunity (2 Corinthians 6.2; Hebrews 4.6-11).

The image of alertness is associated in the New Testament especially with the Church's expectant waiting for the future coming of Christ (e.g. Mark 13.33-37; Luke 12.35-40; 1 Thessalonians 5.2-7; Revelation 16.15). In a different image, believers are not to be like the silly bridesmaids of the parable, who let their lamps go out for lack of oil and miss the one moment for which they have been appointed bridesmaids. The parable teaches the need to be alert, and the folly of not being ready. It is intended to have an impact on our basic attitude to those many opportunities with which we are presented of doing God's will in great or little things. In each of these it is as if God anticipates his final fulfilment of all history. To miss them is as disastrous as missing the arrival of the bridegroom.

From what was said earlier about the place of the Sabbath in creation, it follows that *rest* is a crucial Christian virtue. To achieve an appropriate balance between work and leisure must be a desirable aim for Christian people. Both are essential features of a rounded life, even if the achievement of a proper balance between them is far from easy in a society which has been well described as 'frantic'. However, if believers in Jesus Christ are to give expression to their faith that time is redeemed by Christ, then they will seek to find the right rhythm for the ordering of their lives. They will also want to give expression to the relationship between this balance – of human rest and work – and a due sense of the value of God's creation of the world in time, taking time to value time and to give thanks for it. Worship will therefore be a joyful celebration of the reality and goodness of time, as well as thanksgiving for the redemption which the incarnate God secured by himself becoming involved in time.

Repentance and hope

Repentance is the other side of forgiveness, both as the response to it and as the ground upon which we are able to practise it. It is that temporal virtue which corresponds to the fact that in Jesus Christ, God has intercepted and judged and continues to intercept and judge the structures of human temporality.

The presence of Jesus Christ in the Spirit divides human life into past and future. From the standpoint of his presence, we may look on our past both with gratitude for the constancy and mercy of God and with penitence for what we have made of our own past. Penitence is a way of ensuring that our lives in the past are held up to judgement and therefore forgiveness and absolution. Guilt afflicts human life when we become aware that our past lives and actions are unchangeable and, in one sense, ineradicable, and so that they continue to afflict us in the present; it is often suppressed by attempting to eradicate or evade the reality of the past. Repentance faces the past for what it is shown to be by the light of God's judgement. Yet because repentance involves growth into realistic facing of the past, it also involves a no less realistic hope for a future given through Christ in which we are set free from the tyranny of the past. Repentance is thus a realistic and hopeful way of dealing with the infection of our temporality by sin.

In a culture in which people are suspicious of grand projects, to live in Christian *hope* is to believe that God will finally bring the new world about, in his time. It is to live by faith in a God of newness, who creates out of nothing, conceives a new humanity in the womb of Mary, and (climactically) raises the dead Jesus from the grave. This subverts the notion that the future is the inexorable unwinding of the past. To live in Christian hope does not mean standing in the present and calculating the future; it is to be oriented towards a future of which the raising of Jesus is the sign and the promise, and this means there is the possibility of genuine novelty, surprise.

Humanity cannot expect a steady march of improvement which ignores transience, loss and death. The fact that Christian hope is centred on the raising of a Jesus who had been crucified means that it is a hope which has met the interruptions, infections and discontinuities which evil brings. Hope digs deep. It engages with the worst.

Neither is it the case that hope is 'too heavenly minded to be of earthly use'. Christian hope transforms the present, which through the Spirit makes possible previews of the new world to come. Being caught up in hope now empowers us to live differently, offering the beginnings of vindication and justice to the victims of history.

To live in hope, then, means neither quietism nor feverish impatience. Time is neither to be escaped nor fiercely mastered. There can be a confidence that history is God's, that the outcome is assured, that the timing of the final outcome is not in our hands; and there can be a proper urgency, born of the Spirit, which makes us alert to opportunities to enjoy and make known here and now the life of the world to come.

Wisdom and improvisation

There is an image in Ephesians 5.14-17 which beautifully expresses the virtue of the kind of *wisdom* with which we have been engaging in this report. Quoting from a source now unknown to us the passage says, 'Sleeper, awake! Rise from the dead, and Christ will shine on you.' It then goes on to say, 'Be careful then how you live, not as unwise people but as wise, making the most of the time, because the days are evil. So do not be foolish, but understand what the will of the Lord is.' It is almost as if the 'carefulness' with which the Christians are called to 'walk' – that is, to conduct their lives – is the kind of deliberate step which we sometimes employ when we are bleary-eyed. As far as we are able, we are called to be aware of what is around us, especially in terms of the forces of darkness. As 'children of light' we are invited to walk in the light of the new day which is the day of Christ's resurrection. This carries implications of what was once called 'circumspectness', the careful looking around to see that our steps are sure and that we do not miss our footing.

In Ephesians this exhortation forms the basis for living together in Christian households. So, in the light of Christ, believers are called to a mutual, practical expression of love not only between those members of the household – husbands and wives, parents and children – who are bound by blood and kinship, but also between those – slaves and slave-owners – whose relationship is of economics, power and even ownership. These are moral guidelines, as we would now call them, rooted in a theological understanding of relationships in the present time, which will be over when these 'evil days' are superseded by the coming reign of God. They are not rules to be followed, but attitudes to be cultivated.

So they may make room for the other of this pair of virtues, *improvisation*. To take music as our model, we can highlight two features of musical improvisation.

First, musical improvisation normally involves an interplay between the predictable and the unpredictable. For example, there might be a stable chord pattern, but what a soloist will do with it cannot be foreseen exactly, and part of what we enjoy in listening is the *frisson* that comes from the interaction between what we know is coming and the unforeseeable. To develop the temporal virtue of improvisation means living in a way which does not regard the future as the inexorable unwinding of the past.

Second, commonly, in traditional jazz at least, the soloist takes some given musical material and 'particularizes' it – he or she makes the music live for this particular time, this particular place.

It is here that the ministry of the Holy Spirit especially comes to mind – the Spirit is the supreme improviser, bringing about in our midst particular fulfilments what has already been secured and given in Jesus Christ, for particular times and places. The Spirit now invites us into this process – indeed, being a Christian means being caught up in the Holy Spirit's multiple improvisations.

Improvisation does not mean 'anything goes', a 'free for all'. It means getting to know a past tradition. Traditional jazz falls to bits without interacting deeply with tradition – with the melodies, forms, styles and conventions of the past. There can be no clean slates. Likewise, for Christians to live effectively and relevantly in the present means indwelling not only the irreplaceable tradition of Scripture, but centuries of Christian wisdom – proven traditions of practice, interpretation and belief. This is the way 'originality' comes.

A good improviser also improvises with an eye to the future – trying to sing or play something which will be fruitful, which will lead to other improvisations, hitherto unexplored music. The temporal virtue of improvisation involves 'particularizing' the gospel in a way which gives forethought to the consequences and fruitfulness of our actions.

Chapter 7
The wisdom of love

In this final chapter of the report we return to those common themes which, as we noted in Chapter 2 (pp. 32–33), inform the ways in which the Christian tradition has set out its understanding of human nature. In the immediately preceding chapters we have explored what it means to be human in this particular time and place, as beings powerfully shaped by currents in our cultures relating to power, money, sex and time. We have been concerned to discover the wisdom that points to human flourishing, rooted in the biblical and Christian tradition. We have spoken of this as 'a practical task of contemporary discipleship' (p. 11), something which is best learnt by being put into practice in good habits of mind, heart, imagination and will. But the fact is that the traditions upon which we have been drawing contain within them certain specific teachings which it is now our intention to make explicit by way of conclusion.

The integration of these themes with the way in which we have approached our task can be well illustrated by the biblical tradition of an increasingly personified figure of Wisdom, pre-existing creation and active throughout it. To speak of Christ as 'the wisdom of God' (1 Corinthians 1.24) is to make an extraordinarily important connection. It is to link a practical way of living with a fundamental belief about the author of life. Wisdom is incarnate. In Jesus, the Word, the self-communicating expression of God himself, we see the glory, the character and the very being of the only Son of the Father, full of grace and truth (John 1.14). In the Genesis account of creation human beings are said to be made in the image and likeness of God (Genesis 1.26). The New Testament declares to us what that means by pointing to Christ as the 'image of the invisible God' (Colossians 1.15) and as 'the reflection of God's glory and the exact imprint of God's very being' (Hebrews 1.3). In St John's Gospel, Jesus tells his disciples that to have seen him is to have seen the Father (John 14.9). Yet he is also the one in whom what it is to be human is fully shown. Jesus characteristically referred to himself as the 'Son of Man', a phrase with perhaps a primary reference to 'mortal man', a human being born to die, and yet with overtones of the heavenly figure who comes on the clouds of heaven to redeem and judge the world. When Pilate presents Jesus to the crowd, scourged, and mockingly arrayed in a purple cloak and a crown of thorns, he does so with the words 'Here is the man!' (John 19.5).

The image and likeness of God

The first of the common themes to which we referred relates, in the first place, to the capacity of a person for relationship with God. Two ways of expressing this were familiar: teaching about being made 'in the image and likeness of God', and the doctrine about the soul. Those early Christian writers who shaped the Christian understanding of human nature sometimes distinguished between the 'image' and the 'likeness', saying that whereas we are made in God's image we are only potentially to grow into God's likeness. The distinction, it must be said, has no reliable basis in the text of Genesis; but nonetheless corresponds well to the sense that though human beings are made for relationship with God, they nonetheless have a task in hand if they are to grow into his likeness. St Paul writes to the Christians of Corinth that 'all of us, with unveiled faces, seeing the glory of the Lord as though reflected in a mirror, are being transformed into the same image from one degree of glory to another; for this comes from the Lord, the Spirit' (2 Corinthians 3.18). St Irenaeus in a powerful phrase says that 'the glory of God is a human being truly alive, and the end of human living is the vision of God' (*Adversus Haereses* IV.20.7). But the Christian tradition was also aware that we are born into a 'fallen' world, in which human willing and choosing is flawed. To grow into the likeness of Christ is only possible by grace and repentance, that *metanoia* which is the transforming of our hearts and wills, our mind-set and our choosing, and which is itself a gift of grace.

The teaching about the soul likewise relates to human relationships with God, though here there was considerable ambivalence. The problem concerned Christianity's increasing engagement with Platonic ideas in a world in which Platonism was a dominant philosophy. As we have already remarked, an early and influential teacher, Nemesius of Emesa, was careful to include engagement with this tradition in his exposition of human nature (pp. 28–31). It is easy to give a distorted account of this relationship, as though for example the Jewish world known to Jesus was not already influenced by Platonism. But the difficulty was that, whereas the Jewish Scriptures stressed the full unity of the human person as an embodied self, Platonist anthropology spoke in dualist (body/soul) or tripartite (body/soul/spirit) terminology, with roots in earlier Greek reflection on the *psyche*, the soul, or self, as the core reality of human being. The much more recent developments of psychology and psychiatry may be seen as underlining such an awareness of human selfhood and identity. The word *psyche* is connected with words meaning to blow or breathe, just as *pneuma*, or spirit, is also the word for wind or breath. Of course in the Hebrew Scriptures also man becomes a living being when God breathes into him the breath of life.

One can identify positive and negative features in the encounter with Platonism. On the positive side Platonism recognized the spiritual character of the human person, and human delight in the divine manifest in the world. We identify a negative potential, however, in the tendency to devalue human embodiment, particularly when sharpened by the philosophy and practices of Manichaeism, that movement which identified matter as evil and advocated techniques for the liberation of the spirit.

The resultant model of a human being characteristically places knowing and willing above mere bodily feeling, and sexual experience is relegated to the 'lower nature'. So Augustine, influenced by both Platonism and Manichaeism, could see the passion inherent in sexual relations even within marriage as indicative of the concupiscence that was the consequence of original sin.

The legacy of this separation of reason and will from the affective and embodied side of human nature found a later expression in the Enlightenment, a 'miserable divorce' whose consequences still affect much western thought both Christian and secular. The doctrine of the Incarnation, with its central affirmation of the Word made flesh, has always had the potential to be a powerful corrective to an over-spiritualized understanding of human nature, and the embodied, sacramental character of Christian worship reaffirms this as the shaping of our human nature, individually and corporately, in the likeness of Christ.

Affirming, judging and transforming

A second major theme in the history of the Christian understanding of the human person has been the defence of the idea of the freedom of the will. The main reason for the prominence of this theme is the way in which call and response runs through the whole of the biblical narrative. A previous Report of the Doctrine Commission, *We Believe in God* (1987), has already offered an exposition of this topic (see pp. 122–6). The freedom to respond or not to respond to God is the implication of the narratives of obedience and disobedience which the Scriptures regularly present. But in the process of obedience 'a learning takes place far deeper and more personal than the mental acceptance of propositions, because it is not just a learning but a loving' (p. 123). Loving and knowing God are intimately linked in the Fourth Gospel and the Letters of John. Here the phrase is used, 'resolves to do the will of God' (John 7.17; cf. 1 John 4.7-8; 5.3), expressing a characteristic orientation of human desire.

St Augustine wrote that God has made us for himself and our hearts are restless until they rest in him. We are made in the image of the God of love, whose very being is a communion of love, and who we are is found in our own belonging in that communion of love. Our identity as human persons is never as atomized, isolated individuals. We are who and what we are because we are forged and framed out of relationship, from our very first coming into being through the mutual self-giving of our mothers and fathers. As the nineteenth-century Anglican theologian F. D. Maurice taught, the fundamental relationships of human life, parents and children, brothers and sisters, husbands and wives, are the place where we learn the meaning of love and the disciplines of relatedness that enable us to grow into the wider context of our belonging together in human society in a world-wide community of nations. This approach has more recently emerged in such Jewish philosophers as Levinas, among such Christian philosophers as Ricoeur, and in much Christian trinitarian theology.

For St Augustine, and many Christian teachers after him – not least in the Anglican tradition – the fact that we are made in the image of the God of love means that at the heart of what we are is a desire, which, rightly directed, is a longing for union and communion with the God of love who has made us for himself. We cite again what we have already called 'the most basic wisdom maxim' (p. 13):

> The fear of the Lord is the beginning of wisdom;
> All those who practise it have a good understanding.
> His praise endures for ever. (Psalm 111.10)

We may paraphrase: 'the beginning of wisdom is to live in an awesome awareness of God'. But God, who has created that capacity and desire, has also created us with the freedom for that love and that desire to be directed to other ends, giving to different goals the worth and value that rightly belongs only to God himself. The author of the Book of Wisdom in the Apocrypha writes of the folly of those who failed to 'recognize the artisan while paying heed to his works'. Recognizing the beauty of fire, wind, stars, and rushing water they failed to see that it was 'the author of beauty' who created them (Wisdom 13.1, 3). Later St Augustine could write in his Commentary on Psalm 31 that, paradoxically, all sin springs from love, but of course from misdirected love, the love that misses its true mark, which is one of the root meanings of sin. So what is needful, as Augustine and many subsequent Christian writers on the spiritual life remind us, is that our love is 'set in order' as we are shaped in the likeness of Christ by the grace and presence of the Holy Spirit.

In his *Centuries of Meditations*, the seventeenth-century poet-priest, Thomas Traherne, wrote that 'wants are the ligatures that bind us to God'. He was alerting us to the fact that our desires and our deepest longing(s) are inherent in our being as human persons. If this is the case then even our distorted desires witness to the fundamental orientation of our being to God. The Psalms bear witness to a longing and thirsting for God (Psalm 63.1; Psalm 84.2; Psalm 119.20, 40, 131, 174). In a fallen world distorted desire can dominate and control and it is not surprising that the themes we have particularly studied – money, sex and power – are the places in which our human flourishing can be particularly distorted and corrupted. The particular expression of the Christian life found in the Christian monastic tradition recognizes that in these areas there are particular temptations, which is why the three monastic vows of poverty, chastity and obedience are all concerned with the ways in which the 'unruly wills and passions' of sinful human beings may be ordered and disciplined in these areas. But this *ascesis*, training, the shaping of human life by the grace of the Holy Spirit, is true not just for the monastic tradition but for all Christians who are called to grow up in all things into Christ.

In the midst of life we are in death

In speaking of disordered desire we have already moved into the third common theme of the tradition, namely all that is represented in the narrative of the Fall, and the presence of sin and death in the world. 'The love of the heart ...', Luther taught, 'makes both God and idol.' The love which should be God-directed can become turned in on itself and be directed to other ends and goals. In speaking of the Fall and original sin, the wisdom of the Christian tradition has pointed to a fundamental flaw in human nature, a distortion of the will and a misdirecting of desire. The Old Testament Scriptures warn time and again of the perils of idolatry, first in the worshipping of (the giving ultimate value to) idols of wood and stone, but, more substantially and significantly, in the idolatries that are still dominating and controlling. The biblical 'principalities and powers' can be seen in the oppression of social division, economic power, the politics of violence, the dictatorships and terrorism that are apparent in our contemporary world, and which can be reflected in a myriad lesser ways in the smaller scale of personal and impersonal relationships, including life within the Church.

As it is, our human life, with its desires and potentialities, is always lived towards the horizon of death. The philosopher Martin Heidegger spoke of our human existence as *Sein zum Tode*, a being towards death.

Everyone has the dignity of their own death. The increasing life-span in the 'developed' western world has had the effect of diminishing the sense of earlier generations of a fragile and vulnerable human life in which maternal and infant mortality and a generally shorter span of human life gave death a much more immediate reality. In developed urban societies death is removed into hospitals, geriatric wards and homes for the aged, displaced from the community and intimacy of family and village in the rural communities of earlier ages or of much of the rest of the world today. Death has become the province of experts, both in the medical techniques that strive to keep it more and more at bay, and in the replacing of the traditional ministry of priests and family by the professionalism of funeral directors. What was formerly encountered and celebrated in the public context of community has now become private and personal. Funeral cortèges, which in earlier ages would have been community events, and for which traffic would have stopped, now wend their way to municipal or privatized crematoria through streets of shoppers oblivious to what is passing. *Memento mori*, a mindfulness of death, was once a powerful part of the shaping of human life, a realization of the reality of human mortality, and a means of preparation for what lay beyond that horizon. All religious traditions include within the wisdom they offer for human flourishing an acknowledgement of the reality of death.

Yet untimely catastrophes, sometimes dramatically public, like the events of 11 September 2001, or air disasters, or the loss of life in major earthquakes can bring the reality of death, and our own death, sharply into focus. The public death of iconic figures can act as a catalyst for the relief of more personal, private and unacknowledged or unaddressed grief, as with the death of Diana, Princess of Wales. In a world perspective the terrifying statistics of deaths from HIV/AIDS are a challenge to humanity as a whole, a contemporary instance of the onslaught of the plague that led to the late medieval portrayals of the Dance of Death and associated devotions. In our own society, despite the best efforts of medical science and technology to hold death at bay, they cannot in the end prevent our dying. We may live longer, but we still have to encounter the frailties of old age, and in the end the death that comes to us all.

The Christian Scriptures speak with an astringent realism when they remind us that 'we brought nothing into this world – it is certain we can take nothing out of it' (1 Timothy 6.7). Jesus told a sharp parable about the man who sought to build ever larger barns for the accumulation of his goods only to find that during that very night he would die. Jesus likewise warned that it was perilous to seek to gain the whole world but lose our own souls. In answer to those who tried to trap him by the conundrum of the woman who married in turn seven brothers who all died, and asked whose wife she would be at the resurrection of the dead, Jesus replies that 'when they rise from the dead' men and women 'neither marry nor are given in marriage, but are like angels in heaven' (Mark 12.25). Beyond death there is a new order of life, yet a new order of life which the resurrection of Jesus affirms to be an embodied, yet transfigured, new creation. Money, sex and power are all subverted by the reality of death, and there is a wisdom which comes from 'counting our days', accepting with serenity the limited number of days we are given in which to live, the dimension of temporality and death.

Transformation

The fourth of the common themes of the tradition, that of repentance, forgiveness and transformation, was treated at length in the Doctrine Commission's previous report, *The Mystery of Salvation*. At this point we mention it for the sake of illustrating the integration of themes within Christian thinking. It is an essential part of the Christian understanding of human beings that they are capable of receiving God's grace, that they are able to respond to their situation by repentance, that they can receive God's forgiveness, and through that whole journey, participate in a transfiguration of life. For much of the history of Israel and the Jewish people the dead were thought to go to a place of wraith-like existence in *she'ol*; this was a place not of hope but of life all but evacuated of meaning. Death was the weakest form of life. There was hope of a corporate kind for the ongoing life of the people of God, but no real hope for individual men and women in the face of death. Only gradually did the hope of such life emerge out of the faith that God who had created each human life would vindicate the righteous at that ending of time which was the Last Day, the Day of the Lord, the day of accountability and judgement and the establishment of God's truth in his kingdom of justice, righteousness and peace. The hope was the hope of resurrection, of God's new creation. As God had created the first man, Adam, from the dust of the earth, so there would be resurrection, a new creation. It is a hope given dramatic expression in the prophet Ezekiel's vision of a valley full of dry bones, upon which the prophet is commanded to invoke the life-giving breath or spirit of God (Ezekiel 37).

In the New Testament, Jesus speaks and acts in the consciousness of the imminence of the Day of the Lord, of the coming of the kingdom of God, which is embodied in his person and presence. He shares the hope of resurrection, and lives towards the horizon of his own life in the hope of that resurrection. Indeed in St John's Gospel, where that life is

spoken of as eternal life, he both embodies that life, and in the sign of
the raising of Lazarus speaks of himself as the resurrection and the life.
That was indeed at the very centre of Christian faith, for in the death of
Jesus on the cross God is seen to have entered into the world of sin, of
distorted and idolatrous desire, taking upon himself the consequences of
that sin, not least the blotting out of meaning and purpose that is the
consequence (the 'wages') of sin. The denial of hope that is the reality
of death makes death the last enemy. In the resurrection of Jesus, death
is defeated and overcome. His resurrection is the first-fruits of the new
creation, so that in that resurrection the Last Day has already come.
As Enzo Bianchi has written:

> the death of Christ teaches us how to die and how to live. In the
> Gospels Christ's death is not presented as a fact, a destiny passively
> endured, but rather as an act, the culminating event of a life. It is a
> death brought to life by love – God's love for humanity, the divine
> passion of love that becomes a passion of suffering in the Son's death
> for love.

Living in the power of the Resurrection, we wait with longing
expectation for the 'resurrection of the dead and the life of the world to
come' (in the words of the Nicene Creed).

The risen life

With these last words we have moved to the fifth of the common
themes of Christian teaching about human nature, namely the reality of
a risen life in fellowship with God. St Paul writes of our human
condition as one in which we 'groan inwardly while we wait for
adoption, the redemption of our bodies' (Romans 8.23). For Paul that
liberation is by resurrection, a participation in Christ's own Easter
triumph over death, and a triumph that is both bodily and in the power
of the Spirit. In death the earthly body is laid to rest in the hope of the
life of the new creation, where it will be raised a 'spiritual body' – *soma
pneumatikon*, a body animated by the Holy Spirit. The transfiguration
of Christ's earthly bodiliness in the Resurrection is the paradigm of the
Christian hope in death, though it is true that that hope has also
incorporated elements from the more characteristically Greek outlook,
which has spoken of the immortality of the soul, an understanding that
also found a place in early Christian understanding of the Wisdom
literature of the Old Testament: 'The dust returns to the earth as it was,
and the breath' (or 'spirit') 'returns to God who gave it' (Ecclesiastes
12.7); 'But the souls of the righteous are in the hands of God; and no
torment will ever touch them' (Wisdom 3.1).

The Christian understanding of human nature and human life is, therefore, a calling to share in the Easter life of Christ. In baptism we are plunged (the word *baptizō* means to drench or drown) into the death and resurrection of Christ, being 'born again into a living hope', or, as we might put it, a hope that shapes our living. From the point of our baptism our Christian identity, and therefore our identity as human beings, is to be found in the Paschal mystery in which the God in whose image we are made has chosen to be one with us in our dying and in love and for love to enter into the darkness, alienation and nothingness of death. It is from that point that our humanity has been raised to a new life triumphant over death and hell. In the light of Easter a new creation has been brought into being.

As we have already noted in what we have said about time and redeeming the time, this sharing in the Easter life of Christ has its centre in Christian worship where the reality of past, present and future is brought together in our life in Christ. Above all in the Eucharist, in which we remember and celebrate the passion, death and resurrection of the Lord, we are caught into the movement of his self-offering and sacrifice of love. In this holy sacrament Christ feeds us here and now with his own life, the foretaste of the banquet of heaven, the bread of the Day of the Lord. Here we behold, in St Augustine's words, the mystery of ourselves. We are to be what we receive and receive what we are. Stretching out our hands to receive the eucharistic bread of heaven, we are given our identity and the place where we now belong – the body of Christ. In these holy mysteries we encounter the risen, ascended and glorified Christ who draws our lives into 'the life-time's death in love', into his own offering in selflessness and self-surrender, which he calls us to share.

To live this life deeply and fully, responding to the 'drawing of this love and the voice of this calling' is to witness to a fullness of human life, that stands in judgement over those understandings of human nature, which reduce men and women to consumers, or dissolve the human person in reductionist materialism. The Anglican poet Samuel Taylor Coleridge pointed to the fundamental tension between those explanations of the world and human life that sought to reduce all to the objectivity of 'it is' and those which took seriously the experience of 'I am'. Only the latter could encompass the truth about the human person. Our experience of 'I am' is the experience of a being in relationship and of an openness to grace, which witnesses to the biblical understanding that we are indeed made in the image of the God of love and called to grow into his likeness, the likeness that we see and know in Christ. In that growth misdirected desire will be stripped away in order that we may be enabled to become, in Kierkegaard's words, that person that we are after the image of Christ Jesus our Lord.

In the very first chapter of this report we emphasized that Jesus Christ is our primary reference point for what it means to be human in relation to God, to other people, and to creation. As we have explored the impact on human identity and human flourishing of our being in time, and in that being in time of the shaping forces of money, sex and power, we have sought to engage with the way of wisdom that is ultimately Christ himself, 'the Way, the Truth, and the Life'. Christians are said to be 'in Christ', to be 'very members incorporate' in his mystical body. The life of prayer is a life which the Christian teachers of prayer have seen as moving through the way of purgation, the purification of our motives and desires, to the way of illumination, an ever deeper awareness of the reality of the God of love, to a final fullness of union. St John of the Cross compared this in his *Living Flame of Love* to fire taking hold of dark, damp wood, flickering up in living flames, until the whole log pulsates with the white heat. It is one of many pictures of transfiguration by grace, which is the presence of the living and life-giving Spirit of God. It is that Spirit we ask to transform our lives when we pray 'Come down, O Love Divine!' It is that same transforming love by which we are searched and judged at the end. It is the one thing needful.

> Almighty God, to whom all hearts are open, all desires known, and from whom no secrets are hidden: Cleanse the thoughts of our hearts by the inspiration of your Holy Spirit, that we may perfectly love you, and worthily magnify your holy name; through Christ our Lord. Amen. (Holy Communion, *Common Worship*)

In human life we must all live by faith. Christ calls us to persevere in a way of wisdom in which we are transformed by the lifelong renewal of our minds and hearts. He calls us to a total commitment to God and to our neighbour, the love of God with all our heart and mind and soul and strength, and to the love of our neighbour as ourselves. In responding to that call we will find that such growth in grace demands of us a stripping away and a dispossession. So Paul commended himself to the Christians of Corinth:

> We are treated as imposters, and yet are true; as unknown, and yet are well known; as dying, and see – we are alive; as punished, and yet not killed; as sorrowful, yet always rejoicing; as poor, yet making many rich; as having nothing, and yet possessing everything. (2 Corinthians 6.8-10)

The way of crucifixion/resurrection, which is the way of Christ, can seem a paradox in the eyes of the world, but the love which 'bears all things, believes all things, hopes all things, endures all things' (1 Corinthians 13.7) is the grace which is the key to human flourishing and to that way of eternal life which makes of death the gate of life immortal. It is a life which is no less than deification, a sharing in the divine nature, as we are drawn into the communion of love of the Blessed Trinity, transformed into the likeness of Christ from one degree of glory to another. In the end, as the seventeenth-century writer Sidney Godolphin put it in a poem for Christmas:

> There is no wisdom for the wise
> Save love, the shepherds' sacrifice,
> Wise men, all ways of knowledge past,
> To the shepherds' wisdom come at last.

Index of biblical references

General index